WorldView 3

MICHAEL ROST

Gillie Cunningham   **Sue Mohamed**

Robin Wileman   **Araminta Crace**   **Terra Brockman**

Simon Greenall
Series Editor, British English edition

PEARSON
Longman

WorldView Student Book 3 with Self-Study Audio CD and CD-ROM

Authorized adaptation from the United Kingdom edition entitled *Language to Go*, First Edition, published by Pearson Education Limited publishing under its Longman imprint.
Copyright © 2002 by Pearson Education Limited

American English adaptation published by Pearson Education, Inc. Copyright © 2005.

Pearson Education, 10 Bank Street, White Plains, NY 10606

Editorial director: Pamela Fishman
Project manager: Irene Frankel
Senior development editors: Robin Longshaw, José Antonio Méndez
Vice president, director of design and production: Rhea Banker
Executive managing editor: Linda Moser
Associate managing editor: Mike Kemper
Production editor: Sasha Kintzler
Art director: Elizabeth Carlson
Vice president, director of international marketing: Bruno Paul
Senior manufacturing buyer: Edie Pullman
Text and cover design: Elizabeth Carlson
Photo research: Aerin Csigay
Text composition: Word and Image Design
Text font: 10.5/13pt Utopia and 10/12pt Frutiger Bold

ISBN: 0-13-222330-9

Library of Congress Control Number: 2003065959

Printed in the United States of America
8 9 10 11–V003–13 12 11

Text Credits
Page 21, Good To See You. Words and music by Neil Young. © 1998 Silver Fiddle Music. All rights reserved. Used by permission of Warner Bros. Publications. 59, My Way. Words by Paul Anka, music by Jacques Revaux and Claude Francois. Copyright 1967 Société des Nouvelles Editions Eddie Barclay, Paris, France. Copyright for the U.S.A. and Canada © 1969 Management Agency & Music Publishing, Inc. (BMI) All rights reserved. Used by permission. 97, You've Got a Friend. Words and music by Carole King. © 1971 (Renewed 1999) Colgems-EMI Music Inc. All rights reserved. International copyright secured. Used by permission. 135, If I Could Turn Back Time. Words and music by Diane Warren. ©1989 Realsongs (ASCAP). All rights reserved. Used by permission.

Illustration Credits
Steve Attoe, pp. 5, 66, 102, 106; Paul McCusker, 38, 81; Stephen Quinlan, 20, 96.

Photo Credits
Page 2, David Lees/Getty Images; 4, Robert Frerck/Odyssey; 6, *(top)* ImageState/International Stock, *(bottom)* Omni Photo Communications Inc./Index Stock Imagery, 10, *(A)* Seth Resnick/Stock, Boston Inc./ PictureQuest, *(B)* James Marshall/Corbis, *(C)* Robert Holmes/Corbis, *(D)* Dorota & Mariusz Jarymowicz/Dorling Kindersley Media Library; 12, Yang Liu/Corbis; 13, Getty Images; 15, Stone/Ben Edwards; 18, Spencer Grant/PhotoEdit; 20, Justin Sullivan/Getty Images; 24, Peter Cade/Getty Images; 26, *(left)* Frank Spooner Pictures/Gamma, *(middle)* Britstock-IFA/Wirth, *(right)* South American Pictures/Tony Morrison; 28, The Image Bank/Romilly Lockyer; 29, Andrew Shennan/Getty Images; 30, *(left)* Mary Kate Denny/PhotoEdit, *(right)* Tony Arruza/Getty Images; 31, Larry Gatz/Getty Images; 33, Paul Steel/Corbis; 34, Associated Press, AP/Chris Pizzello; 35, Image State/AGE Fotostock; 36, Siegfried Tauqueur/eStock Photo/PictureQuest; 42, Bob Krist/Corbis; 44, *(top)* Creatas/Creatas/PictureQuest, *(bottom)* First Light; 48, *(left)* IPC, *(right)* Trevor Clifford; 50, *(left)* Abode, *(right)* Abode; 53, *(top)* Associated Press/Simon Thong, *(bottom)* Trevor Clifford; 54, Klaus Lahnstein/Getty Images; 56, Bruce Leighty/Index Stock Imagery; 58, Neal Preston/Corbis; 60, Stone/Jake Rais; 61, *(left)* Corbis Stock Market/Paul Barton, *(right)* Corbis Stock Market/Larry Williams; 64, *(A)* Pictor International, *(B)* The Image Bank/Donata Pizzi, *(C)* Powerstock Zefa, *(G)* Powerstock Zefa, *(H)* Telegraph Colour Library/Ian D. Cartwight; 65, *(D)* Stone/G.D.T., *(E)* Stone/Christopher Bissell, *(F)* The Image Bank/Daniel E. Arsenault Photography; 68, Trevor Clifford; 69, Trevor Clifford; 71, Erlanson Productions/Getty Images; 72, *(left)* Howard Huang/Getty Images, *(left bottom)* Getty Images, *(right)* Zefa Visual Media - Germany/Index Stock Imagery, *(middle)* Michael Keller/Corbis, *(bottom right)* Thomas Del Brase/Getty Images; 73, Corbis Images/PictureQuest; 75, *(left)* Pictor International, *(middle)* Powerstock Zefa/Benelux Press, *(right)* ActionPlus/Neale Haynes; 76, Professional Sport/ImageState-Pictor/PictureQuest; 77, *(left)* Magnum/Peter Marlow, *(right)* Magnum/Peter Marlow; 78, ThinkStock LLC/Index Stock Imagery; 82, *(top left)* Junko Kimura/Getty Images, *(top right)* Terry McCormick/Getty Images, *(bottom)* Steve Mason/Photodisc/PictureQuest; 84, Adam Smith/Getty Images; 86, *(background)* Powerstock Zefa, *(left)* World Pictures, *(A-H)* Trevor Clifford; 88, Glen Allison/Getty Images; 90, *(top right)* Columbia/Sony/The Kobal Collection, *(bottom right)* Stephane Cardinale/Corbis, *(left)* Dreamworks LLC/The Kobal Collection; 92, Digital Vision /Getty Images; 95, Trevor Clifford; 96, Neal Preston/Corbis; 98, *(top right)* Images.com/Corbis, *(bottom left)* Randy Faris/Corbis; 99, *(left)* Stuart McClymont /Getty Images; 104, Bettmann/Corbis; 103, The Bridgeman Art Library/Louvre, Paris, France; 105, Bettmann/Corbis; 107, Gareth Boden; 108, Corbis Images/PictureQuest; 112, Stewart Cohen/Index Stock Imagery; 113, *(left)* Michael Keller/Corbis, *(right)* ITStock Int'l/eStock Photo/PictureQuest; 117, Mark Hunt/Index Stock Imagery; 120, *(top)* Corbis Stock Market/Peter Beek, *(bottom)* Corbis Stock Market/Jon Feingersh; 121, *(right)* Telegraph Picture Library/M. Krasowitz; 123, William Thomas Cain/Getty Images; 126, Digital Vision/Getty Images; 128, Superstock; 130, Digital Vision/Getty Images; 133, *(left)* Bill Bachmann/PhotoEdit, *(middle left)* Richard Klune/Corbis, *(middle right)* Jonathan Nourok/PhotoEdit, *(right)* Forest Johnson/Corbis; 135, Robert Mora/Getty Images.

Introduction

Welcome to *WorldView*, a four-level English course for adults and young adults. *WorldView* builds fluency by exploring a wide range of compelling topics presented from an international perspective. A trademark two-page lesson design, with clear and attainable language goals, ensures that students feel a sense of accomplishment and increased self-confidence in every class.

WorldView's approach to language learning follows a simple and proven **MAP**:
- **M**otivate learning through stimulating content and achievable learning goals.
- **A**nchor language production with strong, focused language presentations.
- **P**ersonalize learning through engaging and communicative speaking activities.

Course components

- **Student Book with Self-Study Audio CD and *WorldView* To Go CD-ROM**
  The **Student Book** contains 28 four-page units; seven Review Units (one after every four units); four World of Music Units (two in each half of the book); Information for Pair and Group Work; a Grammar Reference section; and a Vocabulary list.

  The **Self-Study Audio CD** includes tracks for all pronunciation and listening exercises (or reading texts, in selected units) in the *Student Book*. The *Self-Study Audio CD* can be used with the *Student Book* for self-study and coordinates with the *Workbook* listening and pronunciation exercises.

- The *WorldView* **To Go CD-ROM** offers a rich variety of interactive activities for each unit: vocabulary games, grammar exercises, and model conversations with record-and-compare and role-play features.

- The interleaved **Teacher's Edition** provides step-by-step procedures, exercise answer keys, and a wealth of teacher support: unit Warm-ups, Optional Activities, Extensions, Culture Notes, Background Information, Teaching Tips, Wrap-ups, and extensive Language Notes.

- The **Workbook** has 28 three-page units that correspond to each of the *Student Book* units. Used in conjunction with the *Self-Study Audio CD,* the *Workbook* provides abundant review and practice activities for Vocabulary, Grammar, Listening, and Pronunciation, along with Self-Quizzes after every four units. A Learning Strategies section at the beginning of the *Workbook* helps students to be active learners.

- The **Class Audio Program** is available in either CD or cassette format and contains all the recorded material for in-class use.

- The **Teacher's Resource Book** (with **Testing Audio CD** and **TestGen Software**) has three sections of reproducible material: extra communication activities for in-class use, model writing passages for each *Student Book* writing assignment, and a complete testing program: seven quizzes and two tests, along with scoring guides and answer keys. Also included are an Audio CD for use with the quizzes and tests and an easy-to-use TestGen software CD for customizing the tests.

- The *WorldView* **Video** presents fourteen one-to-four-minute authentic video segments connected to *Student Book* topics. The videos (VHS and DVD) come with a **Video/DVD Workbook and Guide** that includes Lesson Plans, Student Activity Sheets, and Teacher's Notes, all of which can also be downloaded from the *WorldView* **Companion Website**.

- The *WorldView* **Companion Website** (www.longman.com/worldview) provides a variety of teaching support, including model conversations, Video Activity Sheets, and supplemental reading material.

- The *WorldView* **Placement Test** helps teachers place students in the appropriate level of *WorldView*. The placement test package contains detailed instructions, an Audio CD and audioscripts, answer keys, sample essays, rubrics for the speaking and writing tests, and level placement tables.

Unit contents

Each of the 28 units in *WorldView* has seven closely linked sections:
- **Getting started:** a communicative opening exercise that introduces target vocabulary
- **Listening/Reading:** a functional conversation or thematic passage that introduces target grammar
- **Grammar focus:** an exercise sequence that allows students to focus on the new grammar point and to solidify their learning
- **Pronunciation:** stress, rhythm, and intonation practice based on the target vocabulary and grammar
- **Speaking:** an interactive speaking task focused on student production of target vocabulary, grammar, and functional language
- **Writing:** a personalized writing activity that stimulates student production of target vocabulary and grammar
- **Conversation to go:** a concise reminder of the grammar and functional language introduced in the unit

Course length

With its flexible format and course components, *WorldView* responds to a variety of course needs, and is suitable for 70 to 90 hours of classroom instruction. Each unit can be easily expanded by using bonus activities from the *Teacher's Edition*, reproducible activities available in the *Teacher's Resource Book*, linked lessons from the *WorldView Video* program, and supplementary reading assignments in the *WorldView* Companion Website.

Scope and Sequence

UNIT	TITLE	VOCABULARY	LISTENING/READING
UNIT 1 *Page 2*	**Nice to see you again**	Parts of a conversation	Listening: Three people talking about what is happening in their lives
UNIT 2 *Page 6*	**Why women iron**	Adjectives to describe a person's character	Reading: A review of a book about differences between men and women
UNIT 3 *Page 10*	**Living in luxury**	Numbers; hotel facilities	Listening: A conversation about making a reservation for a hotel room
UNIT 4 *Page 14*	**Allergic reactions**	Medical symptoms	Reading: A newspaper article about allergies
Review 1 (Units 1–4) *Page 18*			
World of Music 1 *Page 20*			
UNIT 5 *Page 22*	**A typical day**	Verb and noun combinations	Listening: An interview with a man who has an unusual job
UNIT 6 *Page 26*	**It's absolutely true!**	Adjectives and intensifiers	Listening: A conversation about Carnaval in Rio de Janeiro, Brazil
UNIT 7 *Page 30*	**Eating out**	Adjectives to describe restaurants and food	Reading: A restaurant review
UNIT 8 *Page 34*	**It's a deal!**	Verb and noun combinations	Reading: An article about prenuptial agreements
Review 2 (Units 5–8) *Page 38*			
UNIT 9 *Page 40*	**The river**	Phrasal verbs related to tourism	Listening: A conversation between a travel agent and tourist about a river tour
UNIT 10 *Page 44*	**On the other hand**	Levels of difficulty	Reading: An article on some differences between left- and right-handed people Listening: Two people talking about being left-handed
UNIT 11 *Page 48*	**Trading spaces**	Furniture	Reading: A summary of a TV program episode Listening: People on a TV program reacting to changes in their living room
UNIT 12 *Page 52*	**A soccer fan's website**	Time expressions with *in, on, at,* or no preposition	Reading: A soccer fan's web page and travel plans Listening: A conversation about travel arrangements
Review 3 (Units 9–12) *Page 56*			
World of Music 2 *Page 58*			
UNIT 13 *Page 60*	**Green card**	Immigration	Reading: An immigration officer's interview notes Listening: An immigration officer's interview
UNIT 14 *Page 64*	**What's that noise?**	Sounds people make	Listening: A radio phone-in contest

GRAMMAR FOCUS	PRONUNCIATION	SPEAKING	WRITING
Present continuous for the extended present	Stress on important words in sentences	Making small talk	Write a letter describing what is happening in your life
Comparative adjectives; *as . . . as*	Weak forms: *as, than*	Making comparisons	Compare a man and a woman (or a boy and a girl) you know well
Review: simple present statements and questions	Stress in numbers in *–teen* and *-ty*	Describing places	Write a postcard describing a luxury hotel
Adjectives ending in *-ed* and *-ing*	*-ed* adjective endings	Describing how you feel	Describe a bad cold or allergy and what you did to feel better
Subject and object questions	Locating the focus word in questions and answers	Asking questions	Write an email telling about your typical day
Review: simple past vs. past continuous	Number of syllables and stress in words	Telling stories	Write a true story about something that happened to you
too, enough	Schwa /ə/ in weak syllables, as in *po̱lite*	Describing and giving opinions about food and restaurants	Write a note explaining what menu items to choose and avoid at a restaurant
Modals: *have to/don't have to, must, can't* for obligation and prohibition	*Have to* ("hafta") and *has to* ("hasta") in rapid speech	Expressing obligation, no obligation, and prohibition	Write an informal agreement about rules and obligations
Simple present and present continuous for future	Linking in phrasal verbs	Describing plans for a trip	Write an email telling a friend about plans for a tour
Modal verbs for ability	*can/can't* and *could/couldn't*	Describing abilities and challenges	Describe things you could and couldn't do with your non-dominant hand
Present perfect for indefinite past	Different pronunciations of letter *a*	Talking about changes you can see	Write a letter describing recent changes in your home or life
Modals: *may, might, could* for possibility	Weak forms: prepositions	Talking about possible future arrangements	Write an email telling a friend about possible future plans
Review: present perfect with *for* and *since*	Strong and weak forms of *have* and *has*; contracted *has*	Talking about how long you have done something	Write a report drawing conclusions from two interviews
Modals: *must, might, can't* for deduction	Reduced /t/ in *might be, can't be,* and *must be*	Making deductions	Describe what someone does at a job without naming the job

UNIT	TITLE	VOCABULARY	LISTENING/READING
UNIT 15 *Page 68*	**Mumbai Soap**	Topics for TV soap operas	Reading: Summaries of three parts of a TV soap opera
UNIT 16 *Page 72*	**The message behind the ad**	Adjectives used in advertisements	Reading: An article giving people's reactions to TV ads Listening: A interview with an advertising executive about creating different TV ads
Review 4 (Units 13-16) *Page 76*			
UNIT 17 *Page 78*	**Willpower**	Verbs + gerund; verbs + infinitive to express opinion	Reading: A quiz to evaluate willpower
UNIT 18 *Page 82*	**Wave of the future**	Words related to new trends	Listening: A conversation about a woman's unusual job and how she does it
UNIT 19 *Page 86*	**Made in the U.S.A.**	Materials; possessions	Listening: Tourists talking about items in a shop on Fisherman's Wharf
UNIT 20 *Page 90*	**At the movies**	Types of movies	Listening: An interview with an author of a book about movie facts
Review 5 (Units 17-20) *Page 94*			
World of Music 3 *Page 96*			
UNIT 21 *Page 98*	**How polite are you?**	Phrasal verbs with *turn, switch, go*	Reading: A quiz to evaluate responses to annoying situations
UNIT 22 *Page 102*	**The art of crime**	Words related to crime	Listening: A story about the theft of a famous painting
UNIT 23 *Page 106*	**A balanced life**	Expressions with *take*	Listening: Two people discussing exercise
UNIT 24 *Page 110*	**Digital age**	Technical equipment	Reading: An article about digital TV
Review 6 (Units 21-24) *Page 114*			
UNIT 25 *Page 116*	**Arranged marriages**	Wedding party; expressions with *get*	Listening: Two friends discussing a movie about arranged marriages
UNIT 26 *Page 120*	**Money matters**	Money and banks	Reading: A web page for an online banking service
UNIT 27 *Page 124*	**Less is more**	*Waste, use, spend, save* + noun	Listening: An interview with an author who gives advice on how to find balance in life
UNIT 28 *Page 128*	**Celebrate**	Words related to parties	Reading: An ad for a contest to celebrate a magazine's 100th edition
Review 7 (Units 25-28) *Page 132*			
World of Music 4 *Page 134*			
Information for pair and group work *Page 136*			
Grammar reference *Page 143*			
Vocabulary *Page 151*			

GRAMMAR FOCUS	PRONUNCIATION	SPEAKING	WRITING
will/won't for future predictions	Contractions with *will*	Predicting the future	Predict an episode of a soap opera, a news story, or the result of a sports event
Future real conditional (*If* + simple present + *will*)	Intonation in future real conditional sentences	Talking about future possibilities	Propose ideas for an advertisement to sell a product
Verbs + gerund; verbs + infinitive	Weak forms of *to* in infinitives; blended "wanna" for *want to*	Talking about changing habits	Write a letter describing recent changes in your work or personal life
used to and *would*	Blended pronunciation of *used to* ("useta")	Comparing past and present trends	Compare your lifestyle with that of your parents when they were your age
Passive (simple present)	Syllabic consonants (*cotton, metal*) with no vowel sound	Describing where things come from	Describe a special item you bought on a trip or that someone gave you
so, too, neither, (not) either	Number of syllables and word stress patterns	Talking about favorite movies	Describe what kinds of movies you and a friend or relative like and don't like
Modals: *Could you, Would you, Would you mind . . .?* for polite requests	Weak forms and linking: *could you, would you, couldn't, wouldn't*	Making or responding to requests	Describe an annoying situation and what you did about it
Passive (simple past)	Stress and rhythm in passive sentences	Describing a crime	Write a newspaper article about a real or imaginary crime
Review: verbs for likes/dislikes followed by gerund and/or infinitive	Consonant clusters (*stand, play, sports*)	Discussing work and after-work activities	Write an email about your efforts to balance work and play
Relative clauses with *that, which, who, where*	Stress in nouns and noun phrases	Describing people, places, and things	Describe different kinds of technical equipment you would like to have
It's + adjective/noun + infinitive to express opinion	Different pronunciations of /t/ linked to a following word	Talking about relationships	Write an email giving advice about a marriage problem
Verbs with two objects	Weak pronunciation of object pronouns	Talking about money	Write a letter explaining how you would spend one million dollars
Review: *should/shouldn't, could, ought to* for advice	Reduced forms of *should/ could/ought to*	Giving advice	Write a letter giving advice to a friend or relative about a problem
Present unreal conditional (*If* + simple past + *would* + verb)	Contracted and weak forms of *would* in rapid speech	Talking about imaginary situations	Write an invitation to a party

Nice to see you again

Vocabulary Parts of a conversation
Grammar Present continuous for the extended present
Speaking Making small talk

Getting started

1 **PAIRS.** When we meet someone for the first time, we often make "small talk." What topics do you think are appropriate for small talk?

the other person's appearance	politics	sports
your health your love life	your salary	the weather

2 **Match the sentences to the conversation functions in the box.**

Conversation functions
a. greeting
b. introducing
c. complimenting
d. making conversation (small talk)
e. ending a conversation

1. A: I'd like you to meet my friend, Ana. _b_
   B: _Hi. Nice to meet you._

2. A: See you soon! Say hello to your family for me! ____
   B: _____

3. A: Wonderful dinner! Everything was delicious. ____
   B: _____

4. A: Hi, how are you doing? ____
   B: _____

5. A: It's a beautiful day, isn't it? ____
   B: _____

3 **PAIRS.** Read the responses below. Write the best response under each sentence in Exercise 2.

Yeah! I'm so glad it stopped raining.   Great. How about you?

~~Hi. Nice to meet you.~~   OK, thanks. Bye!

Thanks! I'm glad you enjoyed it.

4 **Listen and check your answers.**

Listening

PAIRS. Look at the photo of Bernardo, Sue, and Tom. Predict which three topics they are going to talk about and circle them.

a death in the family	his or her appearance	cost of his or her clothes
last night's TV programs	school	someone's health
soccer/baseball scores	their jobs	their love lives
their salaries	the weather	why they're there

6 🎧 Listen to Bernardo, Sue, and Tom's conversation. Which topics do they talk about? Check (✓) the topics in the box above. Were your predictions correct?

7 🎧 Listen again and write *T* (true) or *F* (false) after each statement.

1. Sue is surprised to see Tom. T
2. Bernardo and Tom know each other.
3. Tom is Canadian.
4. Sue and Tom worked together.
5. Sue is taking courses for her master's degree.
6. Tom is working in California.
7. Tom wants to see Sue again.

Grammar focus

1 **Look at the examples. Which ones use the present continuous? Put a check (✓) next to them.**

> How **are** you **doing**?
> The sun always **seems** to shine here.
> I**'m visiting** an old friend.
> I **love** the weather in San Diego.

2 **Look at the examples again. Underline the correct words to complete the rules in the chart.**

Present continuous for the extended present

Use the present continuous to talk about **temporary / permanent** situations.

The present continuous is **usually / not usually** used with non-action verbs (for example, *be, know, like*).

Grammar Reference page 143

3 **Underline the correct form of the verb in each sentence.**

1. I **do** / **am doing** fine, thank you. How are you?
2. We **take** / **are taking** a class together this semester.
   We **see** / **are seeing** each other every day.
3. I **study** / **am studying** English for my trip to the U.S.
   I always **have** / **am having** a lot of homework!
4. Josefa **thinks** / **is thinking** about taking an
   accounting class. She **likes** / **is liking** math.
5. I know I **seem** / **'m seeming** tired.
   I **don't sleep** / **'m not sleeping** much
   these days.
6. My brother **lives** / **is living** at home
   until he finds an apartment.
7. They **take** / **'re taking** web design classes
   at the university. They **want** / **are wanting**
   to change careers.
8. Kyung-hee **looks** / **is looking** for a house
   near her job. She **spends** / **is spending**
   two hours commuting each way.

Pronunciation

4 🎧 Listen to the rhythm in these sentences. Notice that the important words are stressed. These words are longer and clearer than the other words.

How are you **do**ing?   **Great! What** about **you**?

So, **how** do you **like** Cali**for**nia?   It's **great**. I **love** the **weath**er here.

It was **good** to **see** you again.   **Why** don't you **give** me a **call**?

5 🎧 Listen again and repeat.

Speaking

6 *PAIRS.* You're at a party. You haven't seen each other in a long time. Talk about what's happening in your lives.

Student A, look at page 136. Student B, look at page 138.

A: *I haven't seen you in a long time. How are you?*
B: *I'm fine, thanks, really busy! I'm . . .*

Writing

7 Write a letter to a friend. Describe what's happening in your life. For example, are you taking any new classes? Are you living in the same place or someplace new? Use the present continuous.

CONVERSATION TO GO

A: What **are** you **doing** these days?
B: Oh, nothing. **I'm** just **hanging out**.

2 Why women iron

Vocabulary Adjectives to describe a person's character
Grammar Comparative adjectives; *as . . . as*
Speaking Making comparisons

Getting started

1 *PAIRS.* **Use the words in the box to complete the sentences.**

aggressive	cooperative	competitive	emotional
~~hardworking~~	messy	noisy	talkative

1. Ben is very __hardworking__. He studies every night.

2. My brother is very _____. He never cleans his room.

3. Marcelo never says anything, but his sister is the opposite. She's very _____.

4. Could you please help? You're not being very _____.

5. Emilia is very _____. She always wants to win.

6. Jack is always getting into fights. He's very _____.

7. I couldn't hear the movie. The people in front of me were too _____.

8. I always cry at weddings. I'm very _____.

2 🎧 **Listen and check your answers.**

3 *PAIRS.* **Describe the people in the photos. Use some adjectives from Exercise 1.**

Reading

4 **PAIRS.** Which adjectives from Exercise 1 do you think usually describe men? Women?

Men	Women
messy	

5 Read the book review. Do the authors of the book *Why Men Don't Iron* agree with you?

Why Men Don't Iron

BOOK OF THE WEEK

by Ann and Bill Moir

Why do women cry more than men? Why do so many men like sports? In their book *Why Men Don't Iron* Ann and Bill Moir answer these questions—and more.

According to the Moirs, the differences between boys and girls are obvious from a very early age. At school, boys are usually messier and more competitive than girls; boys like to win! But girls are often better students. They're more hardworking than boys, and they do more homework. Girls may be more talkative than boys, but boys are noisier. Some doctors believe that baby girls are stronger than baby boys. But by school age, girls aren't as strong as boys.

Why? Does society—our family, friends, and teachers—change us?

A lot of people believe that society teaches boys and girls to behave differently. They say that as adults we can change this. The "new man" should cook, take care of the children, and be more cooperative and less aggressive. He should be neater, more emotional, and a better listener. But are these changes possible? Can men be as emotional as women, for example?

In their book, Ann and Bill Moir say "no." They say that men are more aggressive, more competitive, and messier than women because they are *born* that way. And society can't change their behavior.

6 Read the book review again and answer the questions.

1. What are some differences between the behavior of boys and girls?
2. What do many people believe about these differences? What do the Moirs believe?
3. What do many people think modern men should do?
4. What do you think? Are men and women born with different behaviors or do they learn them?

7 **PAIRS.** Compare your answers.

Grammar focus

1 **Study the examples of comparative adjectives and equatives ([*not*] *as* + adjective + *as*).**

Boys are **stronger than** girls.	= Girls aren't **as strong as** boys.
Boys are more **competitive than** girls.	= Girls aren't **as competitive as** boys.
Boys and girls are both sensitive.	= Boys are **as sensitive as** girls.

2 **Look at the examples again. Match the rule in the chart with the correct information.**

Comparative adjectives and equatives (*as* + adjective + *as*)	
To form comparatives of one-syllable adjectives (e.g., *strong*), _____	a. use *more . . . than*.
To form comparatives of adjectives with two or more syllables (e.g., *tired, talkative, competitive*), _____	b. use the adjective, not the comparative.
In comparative sentences with (*not*) *as . . . as*, _____	c. add *-er* (*than*).
NOTE: Irregular comparatives: good → **better than** / bad → **worse than**	

Grammar Reference page 143

3 **Rewrite the sentences so that they have the same meaning.**

1. Women aren't as messy as men. Men are __messier than women__ .

2. Boys are faster than girls. Girls aren't _____.

3. Girls aren't as noisy as boys. Boys are _____.

4. Men aren't as talkative as women. Women are _____.

5. Men aren't as emotional as women. Women are _____.

6. Women aren't as tall as men. Men are _____.

7. Both girls and boys are hardworking. Boys are _____.

8. Boys are better than girls at soccer. Girls aren't _____.

Pronunciation

4 🎧 **Listen to these sentences from Exercise 1. Notice the short, weak pronunciation of *as* and *than*.**

5 🎧 **Listen again and repeat.**

6 *PAIRS.* **Say a sentence from Exercise 3. Your partner says the sentence that has the same meaning. Take turns.**

A: *Women aren't as tall as men.*
B: *Men are taller than women.*

Speaking

7 **BEFORE YOU SPEAK.** What do you think about the personalities and behavior of women and men in general? Add one more question. Then complete the questionnaire.

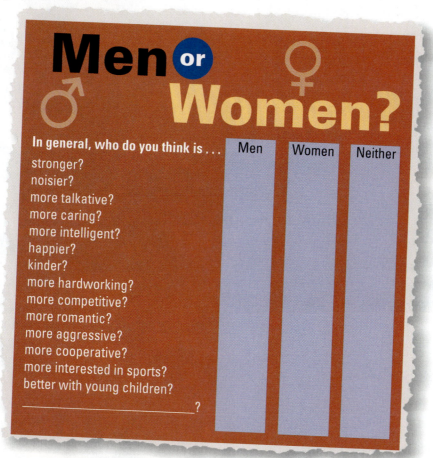

Men or Women?

In general, who do you think is . . .

	Men	Women	Neither
stronger?			
noisier?			
more talkative?			
more caring?			
more intelligent?			
happier?			
kinder?			
more hardworking?			
more competitive?			
more romantic?			
more aggressive?			
more cooperative?			
more interested in sports?			
better with young children?			
_____?			

8 **GROUPS OF 3.** Compare your answers. Talk about any differences in your opinions.

A: I think men are stronger than women.
B: I think they're stronger physically, but I think women are stronger . . .

Writing

9 Think of a man and a woman (or a girl and a boy) you know well. Write a short paragraph comparing them. Use comparative adjectives and *as* + adjective + *as*.

CONVERSATION TO GO

A: He's **stronger** and **more aggressive than** me.
B: But he isn't **as fast as** you!

Living in luxury

Vocabulary Numbers; hotel facilities
Grammar Review: Simple present statements and questions
Speaking Describing places

A

B

C

Getting started

1 *PAIRS.* **Which of these facilities and services can you see in the photos?**

a baby-sitting service	ballrooms	a business center
cafés	casinos	conference rooms
a fitness center	guest rooms	a limousine service
a lobby	restaurants	a sauna
a swimming pool	tennis courts	a video arcade

2 Check (✓) the facilities and services that you think the Four Seasons Hotels offer.

3 🎧 Listen and check your answers. Then listen and repeat.

4 *PAIRS.* Which of the facilities and services in Exercise 1 are the most important to you? Why?

(D)

Listening

5 🎧 **Listen and circle the numbers you hear.**

58	218	385	560
715	719	850	1,217
9,650	13,000	14,850	
140,000		16,000,000	

6 🎧 **Listen to the conversation and answer the questions.**

1. About how many Four Seasons hotels are there in the world?
2. About how many rooms does the Four Seasons hotel chain have?
3. How many employees does the Four Seasons chain have?
4. How much does a premier suite cost per night?
5. How much does a deluxe double room cost per night?

Pronunciation

7 🎧 **Listen. Notice the difference in stress between numbers ending in -teen and -ty.**

eighty   eigh**teen**   **for**ty   four**teen**   **six**ty   six**teen**

8 🎧 **Listen. Now notice how the stress changes when a -teen number comes before another word. Then listen again and repeat.**

eighty **rooms**   **eigh**teen **rooms**

forty **dol**lars   **four**teen **dol**lars

sixty **miles**   **six**teen **miles**

9 🎧 **Listen to the ad and circle the correct number in each sentence.**

1. The hotel is **13 / 30** minutes from the airport.
2. It has **218 / 280** guest rooms.
3. There are **13 / 30** guest suites with balconies.
4. The hotel has **9,615 / 9,650** square feet for dining and dancing.
5. There are **15 / 50** conference rooms.

10 *PAIRS.* **Compare your answers.**

Grammar focus

1 **Look at the examples. Complete the sentences with the auxiliaries *do, does, don't,* or *doesn't*.**

> **(+)** The premier suite **has** a view of the ocean.
> We want to reserve a suite.
>
> **(–)** A double deluxe room _____ **cost** as much as the suite.
> We _____ **need** an absolutely perfect suite.
>
> **(?)** _____ the guest rooms **have** Internet connections?
> How much _____ dinner **cost**?

2 **Look at the examples again. Complete the rules in the chart.**

> **Simple present statements**
>
> Add _____ to the base form of the verb if the subject is
> *he, she,* or *it* in affirmative statements.
>
> Use a form of the auxiliary _____ for negative statements
> and questions.

Grammar Reference page 143

3 **Complete the conversation with the simple present of the verbs in parentheses.**

A: You're at the Four Seasons? What's it like? **(1)** Do you have **(you/have)** a room with a balcony?

B: We **(2)** _____ **(not have)** a balcony, but we **(3)** _____ **(have)** a spectacular ocean view.

A: **(4)** _____ **(your room/have)** a TV?

B: Of course. It **(5)** _____ **(get)** over 100 channels.

A: **(6)** _____ **(the hotel/have)** a swimming pool?

B: Yes, but we **(7)** _____ **(prefer)** the beach.

A: Where **(8)** _____ **(you/eat)**?

B: Usually at a fancy restaurant at the hotel. The waiters are very polite and the food **(9)** _____ **(taste)** great.

A: That sounds wonderful. How much **(10)** _____ **(everything/cost)**?

B: The rooms **(11)** _____ **(cost)** over $500, and dinner is usually over $100.

A: That's expensive!

B: It is, but I **(12)** _____ **(not care)**. It's our honeymoon, after all!

Speaking

4 **_PAIRS._** **You're going on a business trip together. Decide which hotel to stay at, the Delta Hotel or the Marina Hotel. Student A, look at this page. Student B, look at page 136.**

Read the brochure. Then take turns asking and answering questions about the facilities and services at your partner's hotel. Both hotels cost $115 per night. Together, choose one of the hotels.

A: *How many rooms does the Delta Hotel have?*
B: *It has 32 rooms. Does the Marina offer free airport transportation?*

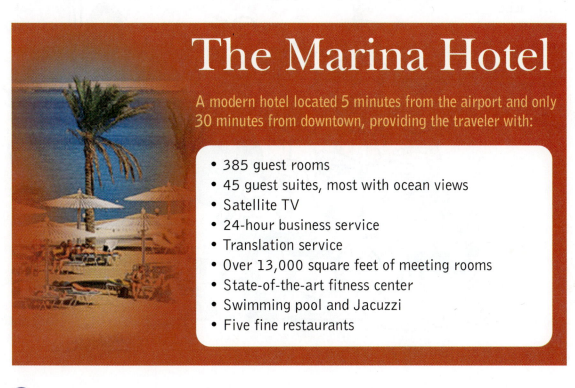

The Marina Hotel

A modern hotel located 5 minutes from the airport and only 30 minutes from downtown, providing the traveler with:

- 385 guest rooms
- 45 guest suites, most with ocean views
- Satellite TV
- 24-hour business service
- Translation service
- Over 13,000 square feet of meeting rooms
- State-of-the-art fitness center
- Swimming pool and Jacuzzi
- Five fine restaurants

5 **GROUPS OF 4.** **Talk about your results. Which hotel did you choose? Why?**

Writing

6 **You are staying at a luxury hotel. Write a postcard to a friend. Describe your hotel. Use the simple present.**

CONVERSATION TO GO

A: **Does** the hotel **have** a fitness center?
B: I **don't know.** But it **has** a nice sauna!

UNIT 4

Allergic reactions

Vocabulary Medical symptoms
Grammar Adjectives ending in *-ed* and *-ing*
Speaking Describing how you feel

Lesson A

Getting started

1 *PAIRS.* **Match the following symptoms with the people in the picture.**

1. a headache __D__
2. a sore throat _____
3. a rash _____
4. a cold _____
5. a backache _____
6. a stomachache _____
7. an earache _____

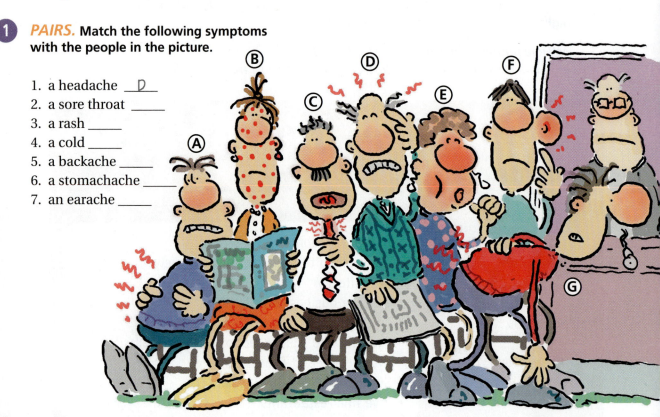

2 🎧 **Listen and check your answers. Then listen and repeat.**

3 *PAIRS.* **What advice would you give each person in the picture? Take turns beginning the conversation. Use a symptom from Exercise 1 and some advice from the list below.**

A: What's the matter?
B: I have a stomachache.
A: Sorry to hear that. You should take it easy. Don't eat anything spicy or oily.

- Don't carry heavy things.
- Have a cup of tea with honey and lemon.
- Sit quietly and try to relax.
- Don't eat anything spicy or oily.
- Take lots of Vitamin C and get plenty of rest.
- Try not to scratch it.
- Don't go swimming.

Reading

4 **PAIRS.** Discuss these questions.

Do you or your friends have allergies?
What are some of the symptoms?

5 Read Doctor Monica's article about allergies and answer the questions.
Which person was:

1. depressed?
2. annoyed?
3. embarrassed?

This week: **Allergy Alert**

Doctor Monica on Call

Allergies are very common and are considered medical conditions. About 40% of the population now shows symptoms of some sort of allergy. Allergies can be very frightening. In the worst case, an allergic reaction can cause death.

Allergies are so common that it's surprising that more people aren't aware of them. Recently a young man named Fabio came into my office complaining of a sore throat and itchy, red eyes. He thought he had a cold. Fabio loves to play sports, and he found it annoying that every time he went outdoors to play sports, his cold got worse. In fact, he did not have a cold at all. Fabio was allergic to the pollen from trees and plants.

A young university student, Silvia, came in the other day to talk about her allergy to animals. Her parents have dogs and cats, and, whenever she's home during school vacation, she gets a rash on her neck and her eyes become red and sore. She said it was embarrassing. Everyone thinks she is crying!

Another patient, Sarah, came to see me about her terrible headaches. She said it was depressing to think that she might have to live with headaches all the time. I found out that Sarah ate a chocolate bar every day. I told her she might be allergic to chocolate. She stopped eating chocolate for two weeks and came back to see me—headache-free.

6 Read the article again. What symptoms did each patient have?
Complete the chart.

Name	Allergic to	Symptoms
Fabio	pollen	
Silvia	animals	
Sarah	chocolate	

Grammar focus

1 **Study the examples of adjectives ending in -ed and -ing.**

> Fabio is **annoyed**. Having allergies is **annoying**.
> Silvia is **embarrassed**. Her red, itchy eyes are **embarrassing**.

2 **Look at the examples again. Underline the correct information to complete the rules in the chart.**

Adjectives ending in -ed and -ing
Adjectives that end in **-ed / -ing** describe how you feel.
Adjectives that end in **-ed / -ing** describe what or who makes you feel this way.

Grammar Reference page 143

3 **Underline the correct adjectives in each conversation.**

1. A: I'm really **<u>surprised</u> / surprising**. I never get colds and now I have one.
   B: It's not **surprised / surprising**. You have a stressful job.
2. A: This rash is really **frustrated / frustrating**. I can't seem to get rid of it.
   B: If you're **frustrated / frustrating**, you should go see a doctor.
3. A: I've just read an **interested / interesting** article on allergies. It says lots of them are caused by pollution.
   B: I know. Politicians should be more **interested / interesting** in the problem.
4. A: I was **shocked / shocking** to hear he's in the hospital.
   B: And nobody in the family has gone to visit. It's **shocked / shocking**.
5. A: She used to hate doctors. Her visits to the doctor were always so **frightened / frightening** to her.
   B: Well, she's not **frightened / frightening** any more. She is a doctor.

Pronunciation

4 🎧 **Listen to the adjectives. Notice the pronunciation of the -ed ending. Write each adjective in the correct sound group. What is the difference between the two sound groups?**

relaxed / bored	excited
tired	disappointed

5 🎧 **Listen and check your answers. Then listen again and repeat.**

6 *PAIRS.* **Practice the conversations in Exercise 3.**

Speaking

7 **PAIRS.** Student A, look at page 137. Student B, look at this page.

You're a doctor. When your patient arrives, ask several questions to find out what the problem is. Write notes below. Offer two pieces of advice.

From the office of _____   Date: _____

Patient's Name: _____

Symptoms:

Writing

8 Think about the worst cold or allergy that you've ever had. Did you receive any good advice from anyone? Write a paragraph about how you felt and what you did to feel better. Use adjectives ending in *-ing* and *-ed*.

CONVERSATION TO GO

A: Life is really **depressing**.
B: Of course you're **depressed**. I'm very expensive.

Unit 1 Nice to see you again

1 🎧 Listen to the model conversation.

2 Talk to your classmates and complete the chart.

3 Report to the class.

Paul is changing his diet. He isn't eating bread or pasta. He's trying to lose weight.

Find someone who is . . .   **Name**

changing his or her diet   _____

looking for a new apartment (or house)   _____

thinking about getting married soon   _____

taking an art class   _____

looking for a new job   _____

going to the gym or health club   _____

not sleeping enough   _____

                                                     _____

Unit 2 Why women iron

4 🎧 Listen to the model conversation.

5 *PAIRS.* Read your point of view below. Have a debate about the differences between men and women. Defend your point of view and give reasons that support it.

Student A, you believe that . . .
- men are stronger than women.
- in general, women are neater and more organized than men. (They usually have to do many more jobs, including housework, childcare, education, and outside work.)

Student B, you believe that . . .
- overall, women are stronger than men. (Men are often physically more powerful, but women have greater endurance and also can handle pain better.)
- men are neater and more organized than women.

6 *GROUPS OF 4.* Discuss your true feelings about differences between men and women. Who do you think is neater, more organized, stronger, more hardworking, or more emotional?

Unit 3 Living in luxury

7 🎧 Listen to the model conversation.

8 *PAIRS.* You are going on a vacation and need to make hotel reservations. Call and ask questions about the hotel's facilities and services. Student A, look at page 141. Student B, look at page 138.

9 Which hotel would you prefer staying at? Why?

Unit 4 Allergic reactions

10 *GROUPS OF 4.* Take turns. Toss a coin (one side = move ahead one space, the other side = move ahead two spaces). When you land on a space, say a sentence with the word. If your sentence is correct, stay there. If not, move back one space.

11 🎧 Listen to the model conversation and play the game.

START	annoyed ➡️	interesting ➡️	frightened ⬇️
worried ⬇️	depressing ⬅️	excited ⬅️	surprising ⬅️
shocked ➡️	boring ➡️	interested ➡️	embarrassing ⬇️
surprised ⬇️	exciting ⬅️	depressed ⬅️	shocking ⬅️
frightening ➡️	embarrassed ➡️	annoying ➡️	FINISH

World of Music *1*

Good to See You

Neil Young

Vocabulary

1 Match the pictures with the phrases.

endless highway __

good to see you __

suitcase in the hallway __

passing on solid line __

Neil Young has been a member of several rock and roll "super-groups"— Buffalo Springfield; Crosby, Stills, Nash & Young; and Crazy Horse. A son of the Canadian prairie, Young's music reflects a sense of country solitude and independence.

Listening

2 **PAIRS.** Listen to the song. Is the singer happy or sad? Why?

3 🎧 Listen to the song again. The lines of the verses are not in the correct order. Write *1*, *2*, *3*, and *4* in front of each line to put them in the correct order.

Good to See You

Good to see you

Good to see you again

Good to see your face again

Good to see you

___ I feel like making up for lost time

___ Now at last I'm home to you

___ I've passed on the solid line

___ I've been down on the endless highway

 2 I'm the footsteps on your floor

 1 I'm the suitcase in your hallway

___ I feel like I know what my life is for

___ When I'm looking down on you

Good to see you

Good to see you again

Good to see your face again

It's good to see you

Good to see you

Good to see you again

Good to see your face again

Good to see you

4 **PAIRS.** Compare your answers.

Speaking

5 **GROUPS OF 3.** Discuss these questions.

What do you like about this song?
The words? The music? The idea?
Do you think a simple song with lyrics that repeat is powerful and effective or repetitive and boring?

UNIT 5

A typical day

Vocabulary Verb and noun combinations
Grammar Subject and object questions
Speaking Asking questions

Lesson A

Getting started

1 Match the verbs in the box with the nouns in the word webs.

~~deliver~~	hire	make	pay
send	spend	take	take out

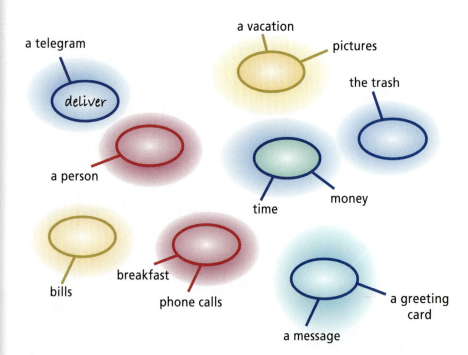

a telegram

deliver

a person

a vacation

pictures

the trash

time money

bills

breakfast

phone calls

a message

a greeting card

2 *PAIRS.* Compare your answers.

3 *PAIRS.* Make five true sentences about yourself. Use verb and noun combinations from Exercise 1. Take turns saying your sentences to your partner.

A: *I like to spend time with my friends on the weekend.*
B: *Me, too. But I only get time to go out with them on Sunday afternoons.*

22

Listening

4 *GROUPS OF 3.* **Tell one another about one of the following:**

- an unusual job you (or someone you know) had
- a memorable party you had or you went to
- a special present you gave or received

A: *My cousin had an unusual job once. He was a bodyguard for a famous singer.*
B: *Really? Who?*

5 🎧 **Listen to the interview with Ron. Can you find Ron and his wife in the picture?**

6 🎧 **Listen again and answer the questions.**

1. What is Ron's job?
2. How much does a singing telegram cost?
3. Who should people call if they want to send a singing telegram?
4. Who pays Ron?
5. What does Ron's wife do to help?

7 *PAIRS.* **Compare your answers.**

Grammar focus

1 Study the examples of subject and object questions.

Subject	Verb	Object
The agency	pays	Ron.

a) **Who** pays Ron?
   The agency.

b) **Who** does the agency *pay*?
   Ron.

2 Look at the examples again. Complete the blanks in the chart with *subject* or *object*.

Subject and object questions using the present simple

In example question a), *who* refers to the _____ of the sentence.

In example question b), *who* refers to the _____ of the sentence.

Use the auxiliary *do/does* in _____ questions.

NOTE: Object questions can ask about the object of a preposition (for example, *with, for, to...*): **Who does** Ron **go** to the parties **with**? His wife.

Grammar Reference page 144

3 Complete the subject and object questions with *who* and the appropriate form of the verbs in parentheses.

A: **(1)** ___Who gets up___ (**get up**) first in your house?
B: Usually I do.
A: And **(2)** _____ (**you/have**) breakfast with?
B: We all have breakfast together.
A: **(3)** _____ (**use**) the Internet the most in your house?
B: My younger brother.
A: **(4)** _____ (**make**) the most phone calls?
B: I do, I think.
A: **(5)** _____ (**you/call**) the most?
B: My friend Judith.
A: **(6)** _____ (**you/spend**) more time with, your friends or your family?
B: My friends, I think.
A: And **(7)** _____ (**spend**) the most time in the house?
B: Not me. That's for sure.

Pronunciation

4 🎧 **Listen. Notice the way the focus word (the most important word) in each sentence stands out. The voice goes up on this word, and the vowel sound is long and clear.**

Who gets up **first** in your house?   Usually **I** do.

5 🎧 **Listen. Circle the focus word in each sentence.**

1. A: Who does the shopping in your house?   B: Usually my father.
2. A: Who does the cooking?   B: My mother does.
3. A: Who pays the bills?   B: My parents both do.
4. A: Who takes out the trash?   B: My older brother.

6 🎧 **Listen again and repeat. Check your answers.**

Speaking

7 ***BEFORE YOU SPEAK.***
Complete the sentences to make true statements about your life.

> 1. _____ make(s) breakfast in my house.
> 2. _____ pay(s) the bills every month.
> 3. Sometimes I help _____ at home.
> 4. I usually have lunch with_____.
> 5. Sometimes I meet _____ after work/school.
> 6. _____ go(es) out for dinner with me once in a while.

8 ***PAIRS.*** **Take turns asking and answering questions about your partner's routines.**

A: *Who makes breakfast in your house?*
B: *My roommate makes coffee, but then we usually buy something to eat on the corner.*

Writing

9 **Write an email to a friend overseas telling about your typical day. Include a few questions about your friend's daily life. Use the simple present and subject and object questions.**

CONVERSATION TO GO

A: **Who uses** the telephone the most in your house?
B: My daughter.
A: **Who does** she **call**?
B: Everyone!

Lesson A

It's absolutely true!

Vocabulary Adjectives and intensifiers
Grammar Review: simple past vs. past continuous
Speaking Telling stories

Getting started

1 **PAIRS.** Match the adjectives that are similar in meaning.

1. bad _a_	2. big ___
3. cold ___	4. crowded ___
5. good ___	6. hot ___
7. interesting ___	8. tired ___

a. awful	b. boiling
c. enormous	d. exhausted
e. fantastic	f. fascinating
g. freezing	h. packed

2 Complete the conversation with pairs of adjectives from Exercise 1.

A: Was the trip really **(1)** _interesting_ ?

B: Yes, it was absolutely **(2)** _fascinating_ ! I had a great time.

A: Was it very **(3)** _____ in Rio?

B: It was absolutely **(4)** _____! Even at night the temperature was over 100°F.

A: Lucky you! The weather here was really **(5)** _____. It was only 25°F.

B: Yeah, I heard it was really **(6)** _____ here.

A: Were the streets very **(7)** _____?

B: Yes, they were really **(8)** _____. I've never seen so many people in my life.

A: Was the music really **(9)** _____?

B: Even better! It was absolutely **(10)** _____! I danced all night long.

A: Were you very **(11)** _____ when you got back to the hotel?

B: Yes, I was really **(12)** _____. I just wanted to sleep.

3 *PAIRS.* Compare your answers.

4 *PAIRS.* Use *very*, *absolutely*, and *really* to complete the rules.

Use the intensifier _____ only with extreme adjectives (like *boiling*).

Use the intensifier _____ only with ordinary adjectives (like *hot*).

Use the intensifier _____ with either kind of adjective.

Pronunciation

5 🎧 Listen to the adjectives from Exercise 1. Notice the number of syllables and the stress. Write each word in the correct group.

○	○ ○	○ ○ ○	○ ○ ○	○ ○ ○ ○
hot	awful			

6 🎧 Listen and check your answers. Then listen again and repeat.

7 *PAIRS.* Practice the conversations in Exercise 2.

Listening

8 *GROUPS OF 3.* Describe the photos of Carnaval in Rio de Janeiro, Brazil. Use some of the adjectives and intensifiers from Exercises 1 and 4.

A: It's really crowded.
B: It looks fascinating!

9 🎧 Listen to Sara talk about her visit to Carnaval. Check (✓) the adjectives in Exercise 1 that you hear.

10 🎧 Listen again and write *T* (true) or *F* (false) after each statement. If the statement is false, write the correct information.

1. Sara went to Rio on a ~~business trip.~~ F—on vacation
2. Sara was in Rio in January.
3. It was raining when she arrived.
4. They were thinking of canceling Carnaval because of the rain.
5. When the rain stopped, Carnaval started.
6. An audience of 70,000 tourists was waiting in the Sambadrome.

6

Grammar focus

1 Look at the examples of the simple past and past continuous tenses.
Underline the verbs in the simple past. Circle the verbs in the past continuous.

> Sara **was visiting** Rio.
> It **was raining** when she **arrived**.
> They **were thinking** of canceling Carnaval because of the rain.
> The weather **changed** and the rain **stopped**.

2 Look at the examples again. Complete the rules with *the simple past* or *the past continuous*.

Simple past vs. past continuous
Use _____ for a situation over a period of time in the past. It often helps set the context in a story.
Use _____ for an action or event that was completed in the past.
Use _____ when a longer action or event was interrupted by an action or event in the simple past.

> **Grammar Reference page 144**

3 Complete each sentence with the correct form of the verb in parentheses. Use the simple past or past continuous.

I went to the Caribbean on vacation this past February. I ___was standing___ in the lobby
 1. (stand)

of my hotel when I _____saw_____ this tall, good-looking guy in jeans and a T-shirt.
 2. (see)

He _____ familiar, and I _____ at him, trying to remember how
 3. (look) **4. (stare)**

I knew him. Then I _____ that other people around me _____
 5. (notice) **6. (look)**

at him, too. I _____ that he was Keanu Reeves, the actor!
 7. (realize)

The other day, I _____ down the street when I _____
 8. (walk) **9. (see)**

some money on the sidewalk. I _____ anyone nearby, so I _____
 10. (not see) **11. (pick)**

up the money: six $50 bills! As I _____ to decide what to do, a young woman
 12. (try)

_____ up the street. She _____ the sidewalk for something, so I
 13. (come) **14. (search)**

_____ her what she _____ for. She said, "I just lost $300!"
 15. (ask) **16. (look)**

Speaking

4 **BEFORE YOU SPEAK.** Think of a true story about yourself. Write notes about the time, place, and what happened.

Possible stories:
- You did something very dangerous.
- You met a famous person.
- You had an accident.
- You went to an unusual place.
- You found something interesting.
- You fell in love.

Time:

Place:

What happened:

_____

_____

_____

_____

5 **PAIRS.** Tell your partner your story.

Last year I went bungee jumping in the Rocky Mountains . . .

Writing

6 Think of a story about yourself. (You can use the story you told in Exercise 5.) Write the story and describe what happened. Use the simple past, past continuous, adjectives, and intensifiers from this unit.

CONVERSATION TO GO

A: We **saw** each other when we **were walking** down the street.
B: **Did** she **look** good?
A: Good? She **looked absolutely fantastic**!

Eating out

Vocabulary Adjectives to describe restaurants and food
Grammar *too, enough*
Speaking Describing and giving opinions about food and restaurants

Getting started

1 **Write the words from the box in the chart.**

bland	~~casual~~	courteous	elegant	formal	greasy
healthful	hot	indifferent	low-fat	nutritious	polite
romantic	rude	salty	sour	spicy	sweet

Type of restaurant	Food flavor	Nutritional value	Service
casual			

2 🎧 **Listen and check your answers.**

3 *PAIRS.* **Discuss the restaurants in the photos and the foods you see. Use as many adjectives from Exercise 1 as you can. Which restaurants and foods do you like?**

A: *This looks like a nice restaurant. It's very elegant.*
B: *It's nice, but I prefer more casual places, like this one.*
A: *What about the food? What's your favorite type of food?*

30

The Palm Restaurant

350 PALM Boulevard

The Palm Restaurant is an old-time favorite with tons of character. The restaurant's spacious, discreetly decorated, and elegant dining room is quiet enough for a business meeting at lunch and also an ideal place for a romantic dinner. If you can, get a table facing the bay.

The employees are courteous and knowledgeable. "You were here last week, right?" a waitress asked me one evening, with a smile of recognition. The chef occasionally walks through the dining room greeting customers.

The Palm serves international cuisine, with varied daily specials. Unfortunately, the menu is already huge and the additional specials make it too complicated for my taste. I ordered from the appetizer menu, which is large enough.

I liked the chicken in a sweet and sour sauce. We sampled the "hot stuff" Mexican appetizers, but they were a little too spicy for some of my guests. The stuffed mushrooms weren't cooked enough, and the fried calamari was too greasy.

As for desserts, there is not enough variety on the dessert menu, but it includes an acceptable cheesecake and a not-so-bad double chocolate cake. The pear in the mixed fruit wasn't ripe enough, making dessert the least appealing part of a less-than-fantastic menu.

Pronunciation

4 🎧 **Listen. Notice the pronunciation of the vowels shown in blue. They all have the short, unclear sound /ə/. Most weak syllables have this vowel sound.**

casual   nutritious   healthful indifferent

5 🎧 **Listen again and repeat.**

6 🎧 **Now listen to these words. Underline the vowels that have the short, unclear sound /ə/.**

polite   formal   elegant   courteous

7 🎧 **Listen again and repeat. Check your answers.**

Reading

8 *GROUPS OF 3.* **What is your favorite restaurant? Why?**

9 **Read the restaurant review. Is the review of the decor, service, and food favorable or negative?**

	Favorable	Negative
Decor		
Service		
Food		

10 *PAIRS.* **Read the review again and answer the questions.**

1. What is wrong with the main menu at the Palm?
2. What did the reviewer think of the appetizers?
3. Would you go to this restaurant after reading the review? Why or why not?

Grammar focus

1 **Study the examples with *enough/not enough* and *too*.**

> This room is **quiet enough** for a business meeting.
> The appetizer was **too spicy** for some people.
> There is**n't enough variety** in the dessert menu.

2 **Look at the examples again. Underline the correct information to complete the rules in the chart.**

(not) enough and *too*
The adjective goes **before / after** *too*.
The adjective goes **before / after** *enough*.
The noun goes **before / after** *enough*.

▶ Grammar Reference page 144

3 **Complete the conversation. Use the words in parentheses with *too* or *enough*.**

Beth: Nice restaurant! But it was _____too loud_____ to have a conversation there.
        1. (loud)

Mike: Yeah, on weekends it's usually _____ for a quiet dinner.
                                            2. (busy)

Beth: Anyway, I had a great time.

Mike: Me, too, although I always find the place a little uncomfortable.

   There isn't _____ between the tables.
                3. (space)

Beth: Stop complaining! There was _____ for two more people
                                        4. (room)

   at our table. And the waiters were great.

Mike: Yes, they were very courteous, but a bit _____ for my taste.
                                                5. (formal)

Beth: They're just polite. You're _____ .
                                    6. (demanding)

Mike: That's not true! I'm easy to please.

Beth: Really? The last time we went to a restaurant you complained all night long.

   You went on and on: "The soup isn't _____ , the coffee is
                                        7. (hot)

   _____ , they don't have _____ to choose from."
   8. (bitter)   **9. (desserts)**

Mike: I never complain about your cooking!

Beth: No, I guess you don't! Maybe I should open a restaurant and call it

   " _____ for Mike!"
   10. (good)

Speaking

4 *PAIRS.* **Role-play. You just ate dinner at a new casual Italian restaurant in your city or town. You both had salad and pizza. Student A, look at this page. Student B, look at page 136.**

Student A, your impressions of the restaurant include:

- a relaxed informal atmosphere
- a nice place for families with kids
- friendly waiters
- great pizza, not too spicy, plenty of cheese on top
- good salad, very fresh, but dressing not sweet enough, too much vinegar
- good selection of drinks
- a little too expensive

With your partner, decide if you would go back to this restaurant again.

A: *I thought the salad was really fresh.*
B: *Yes, but I didn't like the dressing. I thought it was too sweet.*
A: *Really? I didn't think it was sweet enough. It seemed sour to me.*

5 *GROUPS OF 4.* **Think of a restaurant or café near your school. What do you like about the place? Why?**

Writing

6 **A friend from out of town is planning to go to a restaurant where some of the menu items are good and some aren't so good. Write a note telling him or her what to avoid and why.**

CONVERSATION TO GO

A: This place is **too crowded**!
B: You're right. There are**n't enough restaurants** around here.

It's a deal!

Lesson A

Vocabulary Verb + noun combinations
Grammar Modals: *have to/don't have to, must,* and *can't*
for obligation and prohibition
Speaking Expressing obligation, no obligation, and prohibition

Getting started

1 *PAIRS.* **Match the columns to make logical sentences.**

1. When people are under stress, they may *lose* _e_
2. Nowadays, both men and women *do* ___
3. Before they get married, celebrities often *make* ___
4. The way to protect your possessions is to *have* ___
5. People should be responsible and *take care of* ___
6. When you marry someone, you actually *sign* ___
7. It's good to know how your spouse will *react to* ___
8. At weddings, most couples *exchange* ___

a. *the housework.*
b. *problems.*
c. *their financial obligations.*
d. *prenuptial agreements.*
e. *their temper.*
f. *wedding rings.*
g. *a contract.*
h. *some kind of insurance.*

2 🎧 **Listen and check your answers.**

3 *PAIRS.* **Use the expressions in italics in Exercise 1 to make sentences about yourself or people you know.**

I never lose my temper at work, but I often do at home and with friends.

Reading

4 **PAIRS.** **Which of these would you do without a signed agreement? Why?**

- start a business with a friend
- buy a car from a relative
- marry a person you have known for five years
- share an apartment with a close friend

5 **Read the article about prenuptial agreements. Answer these questions.**

1. What is the main reason Hollywood stars make prenuptial agreements?
2. What can prenuptial agreements help make clear?
3. How did Bruce react when Susan asked for a prenuptial agreement?
4. What agreement did Bruce and Susan make?

Legal Terms of Endearment

THESE DAYS, IT SEEMS LIKE Hollywood stars must sign a prenuptial agreement before they exchange wedding rings. The most common reason stars sign these legal contracts is to protect themselves financially in case the marriage ends in divorce. Before Michael Douglas married Catherine Zeta-Jones, they signed a "prenup." If their marriage ends, he must give her $1.5 million for every year they were married. Similar agreements are common among movie stars and very wealthy people.

But times are changing. Prenuptial agreements aren't just for entertainers or millionaires anymore. They can help clarify financial obligations and other responsibilities in any marriage. Bruce Collins and Susan Taylor live in Dayton, Ohio. He is a math teacher, and she is a lawyer. Susan makes a lot more money than Bruce, and Bruce has more free time. So what's in their prenuptial agreement? They agreed that Bruce has to do all the housework and cook dinner. Susan has to pay the bills. And if they get divorced, Bruce can't ask Susan for any money.

"When I first mentioned the prenuptial agreement, he refused to even talk about it. When I insisted, he even lost his temper and accused me of not trusting him," Susan said. "Finally, we reached an agreement because Bruce understood that we're both sensible people. And sensible people have life insurance, car insurance, and homeowner's insurance. So why shouldn't they have marriage insurance?"

6 **GROUPS OF 3.** **Discuss these questions.**

Do you like the idea of prenuptial agreements? Why?
What do you think of the agreement between Michael Douglas and Catherine Zeta-Jones?
What do you think of the agreement between Bruce and Susan?

Grammar focus

1 Study the examples of *have to, don't have to, must,* and *can't.*

> Susan **has to** pay the bills.
> You **don't have to** do any housework.
> Hollywood stars **must** sign prenuptial agreements.
> Bruce **can't** ask Susan for money.

2 Look at the examples again. Complete the chart using *have to, don't have to, must,* and *can't.*

Modals of obligation, no obligation, and prohibition
Use _____ and _____ to say that something is necessary or required. (obligation)
Use _____ to say that something is not necessary. (no obligation)
Use _____ to say *don't do this*. (prohibition)

Grammar Reference page 144

3 Complete the sentences with *have to, don't have to, must,* or *can't.* More than one answer is possible in some cases.

1. You can get married quickly in Las Vegas. After you get the license, you <u>don't have to</u> wait to get married.

2. The bride and groom _____ sign the marriage certificate. If they don't sign it, the certificate isn't legal.

3. When you get married, many people believe that you _____ put your spouse above friends and relatives.

4. In most states in the U.S., you_____ get married until you are 18 years old, unless you have your parents' permission.

5. The state of Mississippi has a different law: you _____ be at least 21 years old to get married, unless you have your parents' permission.

6. In some states, you _____ have two witnesses when you get married. In other states, you only need one witness.

7. Before people can get married in the U.S., they _____ apply for a marriage license.

8. In most states, the couple needs to have a blood test. But they _____ have one if they get married in Nevada.

Pronunciation

4 🎧 **Listen. Notice the pronunciation of** *have to* **("hafta") and** *has to* **("hasta").**

have to   They have to see a lawyer.
                He doesn't have to sign the agreement.
                Do they have to have an agreement?

has to   Bruce has to do the housework.
                Susan has to pay the bills.
                Who has to do the cooking?

5 🎧 **Listen again and repeat.**

Speaking

6 *PAIRS.* **You're going to share an apartment with someone you don't know very well. Student A, look at page 139. Student B, look at page 141. Take notes on the details of your agreement.**

You don't have to go to bed early, but you have to be quiet if you're up after ten, so you can't play loud music then.

7 **GROUPS OF 4.** **Tell one another about your agreements. Is everyone satisfied?**

Agreement between
_____ and _____

I have to:

He or she has to:

I don't have to:

He or she doesn't have to:

I can't:

He or she can't:

Writing

8 **What are the rules and obligations of the neighbors in your community or of the students in your school? Write an informal agreement explaining these rules and obligations. Use modals of obligation, no obligation, and prohibition.**

CONVERSATION TO GO

A: Shh! We **can't** make noise after ten.
B: I know, but we **don't have to** whisper!

Unit 5 A typical day

1 🎧 Listen to the model conversation and look at the pictures on the game board.

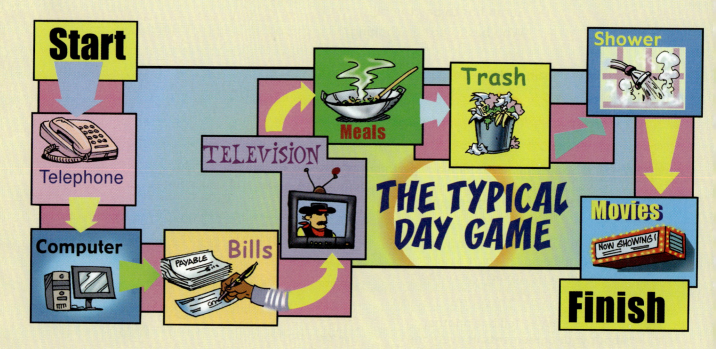

2 **GROUPS OF 4.** Take turns. Toss a coin (one side = move ahead one space, the other side = move ahead two spaces). When you land on a space with a picture, ask your partner two questions about the topic. Your partner answers your questions. If your questions are correct, stay there. If not, move back one space. The winner is the first player to reach the end.

Unit 6 It's absolutely true!

3 🎧 Listen to the model conversation.

4 **GROUPS OF 3.** Read these sentences from the beginning of a story. Write at least two more sentences each to make the story complete.

Barbara was walking her dog one day when suddenly it started raining. The weather was absolutely awful! She didn't know what to do, so she took an umbrella that was leaning against a car.

5 Read your story to the class. Decide whose story is the funniest, the strangest, or the most exciting.

Unit 7 Eating out

6 🎧 Listen to the model conversation.

7 *PAIRS.* You are going out to dinner together. Talk to your partner and decide which restaurant you will go to.

Student A: You're a vegetarian. You have a lot of money, and you like fancy restaurants. You like spicy food from other countries. Think of a few restaurants near your school.

Student B: You like meat, but not fish or vegetables. You like American food. You don't have much money right now, so dinner has to cost less than $10.00.

THE
BLUE LANTERN

Unit 8 It's a deal!

8 🎧 Listen to the model conversation.

9 *PAIRS.* Role-play the following situations.

Student A:

Situation 1. Call Student B and invite him or her to go with you to a great movie tonight.

Situation 2. Listen to Student B's request. Ask him about his rich relative. Tell him you'll have to see a lawyer and sign a contract before you can agree.

Student B:

Situation 1. Listen to Student A's invitation. You have a lot of things to do tonight: cook dinner, do housework, do the laundry, pay the bills, wash your hair, and get to bed early because you have to meet with your boss before work tomorrow.

Situation 2. Call Student A and ask him or her to lend you $10,000 to start a new business. You have a rich relative, but you can't ask him because he's on a world cruise. You have to have the money next week.

UNIT 9

The river

Vocabulary Phrasal verbs related to tourism
Grammar Simple present and present continuous for future
Speaking Describing plans for a trip

Lesson A

Getting started

1 Match the phrasal verbs in bold with the correct definitions.

Phrasal verbs	Definitions
1. They **headed out** at 6:30 in the morning. _g_	a. take someone to different parts of a new place to point out what is important or interesting
2. My friends **put** me **up** for two nights. ___	
3. She **got off** the bus at the last stop. ___	b. stopped working (used with machines)
4. The car **broke down**, so I called the mechanic. ___	c. left a plane, train, boat, etc.
5. The train stopped briefly, and then **went on** to the next station. ___	d. began a trip at a particular place
	e. continued traveling after a stop
6. We **started off** on High Street. ___	f. let someone stay in your home for a short time
7. We hired a tour guide to **show** us **around** London. ___	g. left at a specified time to go someplace or do something

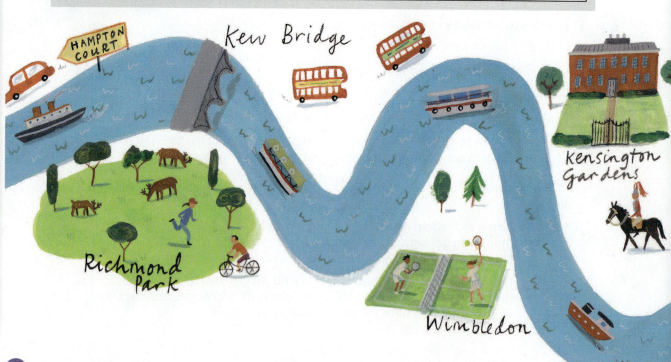

2 **PAIRS.** Take turns describing an interesting trip you have taken (for example, a school trip, a weekend away, or a vacation). Use some of the phrasal verbs in Exercise 1.

Last summer, my family and I went camping. We headed out at six on a Friday morning . . .

Listening

3 **PAIRS.** **Look at the map of the River Thames in London. Discuss these questions.**

Which places would you like to visit?
When you visit a new place, do you like having someone show you around,
or do you like to explore on your own? Why?

4 🎧 **Listen to the conversation between a tourist and a travel agent. Check (✓)
the places on the map that they mention.**

5 🎧 **Listen again and answer the questions.**

1. What time does the tour start on the first day?
2. What time do they get off at Hampton Court?
3. What is the tourist doing the first evening?
4. What is the tourist doing the second evening?

Grammar focus

1 Look at the examples of the simple present and present continuous tenses. Write *simple present* or *present continuous* next to each one.

a. The tour **starts** at nine on Monday.
b. I'**m meeting** a friend for dinner.
c. What time **does** the boat **head out**?
d. I'**m going** to the theater tonight.

2 Look at the examples again. Underline the correct information to complete the rules in the chart. Then match the examples with the rules.

> **Simple present and present continuous for future**
>
> Use the **simple present / present continuous** to talk about schedules, timetables, and events on the calendar in the future. Example sentences __ and __.
>
> Use the **simple present / present continuous** to talk about personal plans in the future. Example sentences __ and __.

> *Grammar Reference page 145*

3 Complete the sentences with the correct form of the simple present or present continuous for the future.

1. The tour ___ starts off ___ (**start off**) at Washington Square Park.
2. The movie _____ (**begin**) at seven tonight.
3. What _____ (**you/do**) this evening?
4. The semester _____ (**end**) on June 15.
5. Mike _____ (**come**) to see us tomorrow morning.
6. Where _____ (**they/go**) on vacation this summer?
7. I _____ (**work**) until four tomorrow.

Pronunciation

4 🎧 Listen to the phrasal verbs. Notice how a consonant or vowel sound at the end of a word is linked to a vowel sound at the beginning of the next word.

head out	When does the boat head out?
get off	We get off at Hampton Court.
show us around	A guide will show us around.
go on	Then we go on to the park.
putting me up	A friend is putting me up.

5 🎧 Listen again and repeat.

Speaking

6 **PAIRS.** Imagine you're taking a weekend trip together to Washington, D.C. Student A, look at page 137. Student B, look at page 139.

7 **PAIRS.** Look at the brochure about Washington, D.C. Use the information to plan your weekend. Include places to go, places to eat, and the times for each activity. Take notes for both Saturday and Sunday.

A: *OK, on Saturday, do you want to go dancing or go to dinner somewhere?*
B: *Let's do both. Let's eat dinner at about 7:30 at Star of Siam and then go to the Black Cat Club.*

WASHINGTON, D.C.: Weekend activities

PLACES TO VISIT	TOURS
• The U.S. Capitol Building	• D.C. Heritage Walking Tour (3 hours)
• The Lincoln Memorial	• Canal Boat Ride on the Chesapeake Canal (1 hour)
• The Washington Monument	• Bus Tour of Washington ($1\frac{1}{2}$ hours)
• The National Air and Space Museum	• White House Tour ($1\frac{1}{2}$ hours)
• The National Zoo	
• The National Museum of Art	

RESTAURANTS	NIGHTLIFE
• Pizzeria Paradiso (Italian food)	• Alvin Ailey American Dance Theatre at the Kennedy Center
• Five Guys (American food)	• Opera at Constitution Hall
• Restaurant Nora (Organic/natural food)	• Blues (music) at the Zoo Bar Café
• Star of Siam (Thai food)	• Dancing at the Black Cat Club

8 **GROUPS OF 4.** Tell each other what you're planning to do on Saturday and Sunday. Find out if you are doing any of the same things at the same time.

On Saturday, we're heading out early and having a quick breakfast near our hotel. Then we're taking a walking tour. At about 12:00, we're having lunch at . . .

Writing

9 You want a friend to join you on your trip. Write an email telling your friend about your plans. Use the simple present and present continuous for future.

CONVERSATION TO GO

A: What time **does** the tour **start**?
B: It **starts** at 9:00, but we**'re meeting** at 8:30. Don't be late!

On the other hand

Vocabulary	Levels of difficulty
Grammar	Modal verbs for ability
Speaking	Describing abilities and challenges

Lesson A

Getting started

1 **PAIRS.** Write the expressions from the box in the correct columns.

a piece of cake	challenging	complicated	doable
hard	impossible	manageable	no trouble
simple	straightforward	tough	

It was . . .

Easy	OK	Difficult
a piece of cake	doable	challenging

2 🎧 Listen and check your answers. Then listen and repeat.

3 **PAIRS.** Discuss how you felt when you first learned to do three of these things. Use the expressions in Exercise 1.

drive a car	program a VCR	ride a bicycle
speak English	take care of a baby	use the Internet

A: *How did you feel when you first learned to drive a car?*
B: *It was impossible at the beginning, but then it became manageable.*

Reading

4 **PAIRS.** Discuss these questions.

Do you know anyone who is left-handed?
Do you know anyone who is ambidextrous?
Are most people you know righties or lefties?

5 Read the article and answer the questions.

1. Who uses the "other" hand more often, lefties or righties? Why?
2. What is the advantage of being ambidextrous over being left-handed?

Can Lefties Do It Right?

Leonardo da Vinci, Marilyn Monroe, Paul McCartney, Pelé, Bill Gates . . . what do all these people have in common? They are all left-handed!

Being left-handed means that you find it more straightforward to do things with your left hand than with your right. It may also mean that you prefer to use your left foot or left eye (for example, with a camera).

Depending on how you define it, between 10% and 30% of people are left-handed. But most left-handers use their right hand for at least some things —like shaking hands.

Some people can do things with both hands equally well. Being ambidextrous is a big advantage over being a lefty, because we live in a world designed for right-handed people. Tools, sports equipment, and many musical instruments are designed for people who are right-handed.

If you are a lefty, take heart. Many famous lefties have risen above these challenges and succeeded, as Leonardo, Marilyn, Paul, Pelé, and Bill have shown.

Listening

6 🎧 Mike and Juliana are talking about being left-handed. Listen to the first part of their conversation. Check (✓) the things they mention.

___ writing   ___ cutting   ___ drawing   ___ kicking

7 🎧 Look at the pictures of the ability tests that Mike and Juliana did with their right hands. Listen to the rest of their conversation. How hard was each test? Write *M* for Mike or *J* for Juliana next to each result.

___ pretty easy   ___ not too difficult   ___ more manageable with right   ___ pretty simple

___ a piece of cake   ___ really challenging   ___ more straightforward with right   ___ complicated

Grammar focus

1 **Study the examples of modals of ability.**

She **can** play the piano really well.	I was surprised that I **was able to** win that race.
I **couldn't** cook until I got married.	I **managed to** get an A in math.
He **could** play chess when he was four.	We **didn't manage to** get tickets to the opera.
He **was able to** use a computer when he was five.	They **weren't able to** make reservations.

2 **Look at the examples again. Complete the rules in the chart using *can (not),* *could (not), (not) be able to,* or *(not) manage to.***

Modals of ability: *can, could, be able to, manage to*

Use _____ to talk about ability in the present.

Use _____ or _____ to talk about a permanent ability in the past.

Use _____ or _____ (but not *could*) to talk about something that was possible at a specific time in the past.

Use _____ or _____ or _____ to talk about something that was not possible at a specific time in the past.

> *Grammar Reference page 145*

3 **Complete the sentences using the correct form of *can, could, be able to,* or *manage to.* Use each form at least once. Some sentences have more than one correct answer.**

1. The homework was difficult, but in the end I ___managed to___ do it.

2. Sara broke her leg last year, but she _____ walk just fine now.

3. Kyoko missed the train to the airport, but she _____ get a bus and arrived just in time for her flight.

4. When I was four, I _____ read all by myself.

5. I _____ save enough money for a new car, so I bought a used one.

6. My writing has improved, so I _____ pass the English test.

7. I took dance lessons this spring. Now I _____ dance to salsa music.

8. Tom locked his keys in the car with the keys inside, but he _____ open the door anyway.

9. Kim _____ fix her computer, so she called a technician.

10. I _____ tie my shoes until I was eight years old.

Pronunciation

4 🎧 **Listen.** Notice the short, weak pronunciation of *can* and *could* and the stronger pronunciation of *can't* and *couldn't* in these sentences.

She can throw a ball with either hand.

He could play chess when he was four.

I **can't** draw with my left hand.

I **couldn't** cook until I got married.

5 🎧 **Listen again and repeat.**

6 🎧 **Listen. Write the word you hear in each sentence:** *can, can't, could,* or *couldn't.*

1. They ___can___ dance very well.

2. She _____ ride a bike.

3. He _____ play the guitar.

4. My grandmother _____ speak English.

5. I _____ read without glasses.

6. He _____ write with his left hand.

Speaking

7 *BEFORE YOU SPEAK.* **Do the ability tests in the chart. Use your "other" hand. Take notes in the chart.**

8 *PAIRS.* **Take turns. Tell each other how you did on the ability tests.**

A: *I was able to write* have fun, *but no one could read it!*

B: *I couldn't write with my left hand. It was impossible!*

> throw a paper ball into a wastepaper basket
>
> ....
>
> write the words "have fun"
>
> ....
>
> flip and catch a coin
>
> ....
>
> draw a face
>
> ....

Writing

9 **Write a brief report describing your results on the ability tests. Were you surprised by your results? Use** *can, could, be able to,* **and** *manage to.*

CONVERSATION TO GO

A: Did you **manage to** fix the car?
B: Yes, it was **a piece of cake**!

Trading spaces

Vocabulary Furniture
Grammar Present perfect for indefinite past
Speaking Talking about changes you can see

Getting started

1 **PAIRS.** Match the words with the furniture and other items in the photo.

armchair __m__   basket ____   bookcase ____   cabinet ____

carpet ____   drapes ____   fireplace ____   lamp ____

magazine rack ____   plants ____   picture ____   rug ____

sofa ____   stereo speakers ___   throw pillow ____   window ____

2 Match the sentences with the responses.

1. I don't like the sofa that color. __e__
2. That window needs some drapes. ____
3. The cabinet looks terrible there. ____
4. The floor in this room looks old. ____
5. That throw pillow on the arm chair is ugly. ____

a. You're right. Let's make some.
b. Why don't we refinish it?
c. Let's throw it out and get a new one.
d. Let's move it to the other side of the room.
e. Me, neither. Why don't we cover it?

3 **PAIRS.** Share your opinions about the room in the photo.

Pronunciation

4 🎧 **Listen. Notice the pronunciation of the letter *a* in each word.**

magazine	table	art

5 *PAIRS.* **How is the letter *a* pronounced in the following words? Write each word in the correct sound group.**

armchair   basket   bookcase   cabinet   carpet

drapes   fireplace   lamp   plants   rack

6 🎧 **Listen and check your answers. Then listen and repeat.**

Reading

7 **Read about the program "Trading Spaces" in *TV Choice* and answer these questions.**

1. What is the relationship between the Macedos and the Nelsons?
2. What are the two couples doing?
3. How much time and money do they have? .

TV Choice

This week on "Trading Spaces," two pairs of neighbors, Pedro and Carla Macedo and John and Cassie Nelson, work with professional designers to completely redecorate a room in each other's home. They have two days and a budget of $1,000 each. When the Macedos and Nelsons return to their own homes, will they be pleased or angry? Watch "Trading Spaces" on Tuesday evening at 8:00 to find out.

Listening

8 🎧 **Listen to Carla and Pedro's reactions to their new living room. Who likes the room more, Carla or Pedro?**

9 🎧 **Listen again. Match the columns to describe what the Nelsons have done to the Macedos' living room.**

1. They've thrown away ____   a. the sofa.
2. They've painted ____   b. covers and throw pillows for the armchairs.
3. They've made ____   c. the walls red.
4. They've moved ____   d. new drapes.
5. They've bought ____   e. the bookcase.
6. They've put ____   f. the books in the cabinet.

Grammar focus

1 **Study the examples of present perfect for the indefinite past.**

What **have** they **done**?	They**'ve painted** the walls bright red.
What **has** he **made**?	He**'s made** new drapes.
Has she **bought** new armchairs?	No, she **hasn't**.

2 **Look at the examples again. Underline the correct words to complete the explanations in the chart.**

Present perfect for indefinite past

Use the present perfect to describe a **present / past** action.

The time of the action **is / is not** important.

> *Grammar Reference page 145*

Before

3 **The Nelsons are looking at the kitchen that the Macedos have just remodeled. Use the present perfect form of the verbs in the box to complete the conversation. Sometimes more than one answer is correct.**

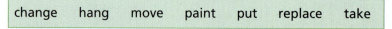

change   hang   move   paint   put   replace   take

Announcer: Hi, Cassie. Hi, John. Look at your new kitchen!

Cassie: Wow! Our neighbors Pedro and Carla

(1) _have changed_ everything.

John: Yes, I see Pedro (2) _____ the stove over to

this wall . . . and are those new kitchen cabinets?

Announcer: Yes, Pedro and Cassie (3) _____ them

all, and they (4) _____ them all gray.

Cassie: I love the cabinets . . . , but what happened to the

washing machine?

After

Announcer: Pedro (5) _____ it to the basement.

John: And over on that wall? What's all that?

Announcer: That was Carla's idea. She (6) _____ all the pots and pans up there.

I think that's really handy.

Cassie: And the floor. There's something different about the floor.

John: Yes, they (7) _____ the floor, too. It now has beautiful red tiles. It feels

like we have a whole new kitchen!

Speaking

4 *PAIRS*. **A team of designers has just redecorated this room. Look at the *before* and *after* photos and find the six changes the design team has made. You have five minutes. Take notes.**

A: *They've painted the walls green.*
B: *Right. And they've changed the drapes.*

Before

After

5 *GROUPS OF 4.* **Compare your notes. Have you found the same six changes?**

6 **Do you like the changes? Are there any different changes you would make?**

Writing

7 **Write a letter to a friend. Describe recent changes you have made either in your home or in your life. You can use your imagination. Use the present perfect for indefinite past.**

CONVERSATION TO GO

A: **Have you decorated** the house?
B: We**'ve painted** the walls, but we **haven't done** anything else.

A soccer fan's website

Vocabulary Time expressions with *in, on, at,* or no preposition
Grammar Modals: *may, might, could* for possibility
Speaking Talking about possible future arrangements

Lesson A

Getting started

1 **PAIRS. Write the time expressions in the correct columns.**

last Friday afternoon	the evening	Thursday
next Monday evening	the morning	yesterday morning
noon	this Thursday	6:45 P.M.

in	on	at	no preposition
			last Friday afternoon

2 🎧 **Listen and check your answers.**

3 **PAIRS. Complete the sentences with a preposition where necessary.**

1. I met Josephine for lunch __at__ noon.
2. Where were you _____ last night?
3. Pedro came home _____ 4 A.M.
4. I might go to a soccer game _____ Saturday afternoon.
5. Su-ki may phone you _____ the evening.
6. Did you see Yori _____ yesterday evening?
7. Her plane left _____ midnight.
8. I have to go to soccer practice _____ Monday.

Pronunciation

4 🎧 **Listen. Notice the weak pronunciation of the prepositions *at, in,* and *on*.**

We're leaving at ten.   We arrive at four in the afternoon.
We can walk around in the morning.   There's a tour at noon on Sunday.
I think I'll go shopping on Tuesday.   Let's meet at our hotel in the evening.

5 🎧 **Listen again and repeat.**

6 **PAIRS. Take turns reading the sentences in Exercise 3.**

Reading

7 *PAIRS.* **Manchester United is a well-known sports team. The sport is called _____ in the U.S. and _____ in most other English-speaking countries.**

8 **Peter is a big fan of Manchester United. Read his web page and answer the questions.**

1. Which three cities is Peter planning to visit?
2. How many games is he going to?
3. How long is the trip?

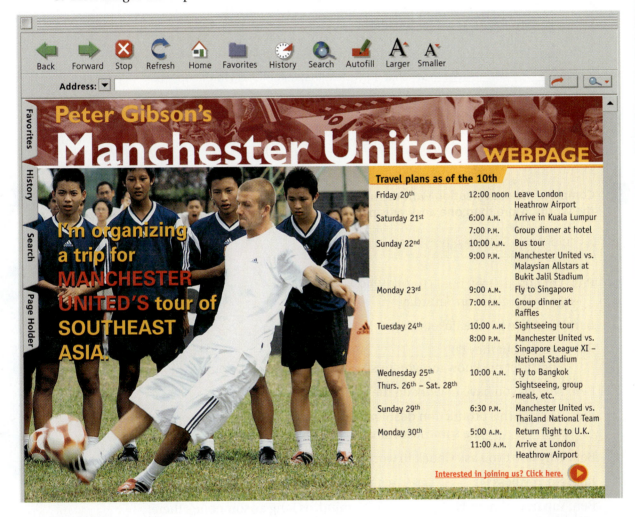

Back	Forward	Stop	Refresh	Home	Favorites	History	Search	Autofill	Larger	Smaller

Address: ▼

Peter Gibson's
Manchester United WEBPAGE

I'm organizing a trip for MANCHESTER UNITED'S tour of SOUTHEAST ASIA.

Travel plans as of the 10th

Friday 20th	12:00 noon	Leave London Heathrow Airport
Saturday 21st	6:00 A.M.	Arrive in Kuala Lumpur
	7:00 P.M.	Group dinner at hotel
Sunday 22nd	10:00 A.M.	Bus tour
	9:00 P.M.	Manchester United vs. Malaysian Allstars at Bukit Jalil Stadium
Monday 23rd	9:00 A.M.	Fly to Singapore
	7:00 P.M.	Group dinner at Raffles
Tuesday 24th	10:00 A.M.	Sightseeing tour
	8:00 P.M.	Manchester United vs. Singapore League XI – National Stadium
Wednesday 25th	10:00 A.M.	Fly to Bangkok
Thurs. 26th – Sat. 28th		Sightseeing, group meals, etc.
Sunday 29th	6:30 P.M.	Manchester United vs. Thailand National Team
Monday 30th	5:00 A.M.	Return flight to U.K.
	11:00 A.M.	Arrive at London Heathrow Airport

Interested in joining us? Click here. ▶

Listening

9 🎧 **Listen to Peter's phone conversation with another fan. Circle the information on the web page that might change.**

10 🎧 **Listen again and answer the questions.**

1. Why is Peter calling Charles?
2. What is the problem with the dinner at Raffles?
3. Does Charles think that a shopping trip is a good idea? Why?

Grammar focus

1 **Study the examples of modals of possibility.**

It **could** be difficult to get a taxi.	Some people **may not** go sightseeing.
We **could** arrive late at night.	We **might** leave at ten o'clock.
You **may** need to get up earlier.	We **might not** take a bus.

2 **Look at the examples again. Fill in the blanks in the chart with** *may, may not, might, might not, could,* **and** *couldn't.*

Modals: *may, might, could* for possibility

Use _____ , _____ , or _____ when it is possible that something will happen.

Use _____ or _____ when it is possible that something won't happen.

Use _____ when it is impossible that something will happen.

> *Grammar Reference page 146*

3 **Complete the conversation with the appropriate form of the words. More than one answer is possible in some cases.**

could (not)	may (not)	might (not)

Rob: I'm not sure yet, but I **(1)** __may not__ be able to go to the game on Saturday.

Ben: Why? I've got the tickets already!

Rob: I know, but they **(2)** _____ need me at work. They'll let me know tonight for sure.

Ben: Why do you have to work on the weekend?

Rob: We have this production deadline, and there **(3)** _____ be some last-minute changes.

Ben: Why don't you ask Chuck to work for you?

Rob: No, my boss **(4)** _____ get upset. I **(5)** _____ do that.

Ben: You never know. He **(6)** _____ mind, as long as someone's there!

Rob: Besides, Chuck **(7)** _____ have things to do on Saturday.

Ben: Or he **(8)** _____. You never know. He **(9)** _____ be free.

Rob: OK, let me call him. Chuck? Hi! It's me, Rob. I have a huge favor to ask. There's this game on Saturday, but I **(10)** _____ be able to go because I **(11)** _____ have to go to the office, and . . . OK, thank you.

Ben: What did he say?

Rob: He said yes, but he also said he **(12)** _____ ask me to work for him next weekend. I guess it's only fair!

Speaking

4 *BEFORE YOU SPEAK.* Complete the calendar page with four of the activities on the list, or add your own ideas. Include two activities that you might do, and two activities that you plan to do. Be sure to leave at least three hours open during the afternoon or evening.

- go to the gym
- visit my (relative)
- go shopping
- clean the house
- have coffee with (name)
- get a haircut

DAILY PLANNER

Saturday

11:00 A.M.	6:00 P.M.
12:00 P.M.	7:00 P.M.
1:00 P.M.	8:00 P.M.
2:00 P.M.	9:00 P.M.
3:00 P.M.	10:00 P.M.
4:00 P.M.	11:00 P.M.
5:00 P.M.	

5 *PAIRS.* Find a time to meet on Saturday to go to a movie together. You need to get to the theater at least half an hour before the show.

A: *Are you free on Saturday afternoon? I thought we could go to a movie.*
B: *Sure, what time?*
A: *What about two?*
B: *Well, I might have coffee with my friend Sarah at 1:30…*

PLAZA 3
555-6101
Show times:
12:00 P.M., 2:30 P.M., 4:40 P.M.,
7:10 P.M., 10:00 P.M.

Writing

6 Write a short email to a friend describing all the things you may/might/could do in the next few weeks or months. Use the modals for possibility.

CONVERSATION TO GO

A: I heard you **might not** go to the soccer game tomorrow.
B: If I get this work done tonight, I **may** go after all.

Review 3 — Units 9–12

Unit 9 The river

1. 🎧 Listen to the model conversation.

2. **BEFORE YOU SPEAK.** Look at the brochure for the Chicago Trolley Tour. Pick three places that you'd like to visit and circle them.

3. **GROUPS OF 3.** Work together to plan your group's visit to Chicago. You probably won't be able to visit all the places that the Chicago Trolley Tour goes to. Agree on the places you'd like to visit and how long you'll stay at each place.

TOUR SCHEDULE:

Daily—9 A.M. to 4:30 P.M. The first trolley heads out at 9 A.M. sharp. You can get on and off the trolley at any stop. Tour guides can show you around at many locations. The tour takes about three hours, but you can skip some stops and stay longer at others.

Boarding Locations/Stops:

* Sears Tower: Chicago's tallest building
* Marshall Field's: a grand old department store
* Chicago River South: take a walk along the beautiful Chicago River
* Art Institute: see our world-famous art museum
* Museum Campus: (includes the Field Museum of Natural History, the Shedd Aquarium, and the Adler Planetarium)
* Navy Pier: for great food, shopping, and entertainment
* Water Tower: the historic stone building that survived the Chicago Fire
* Rainforest Cafe: take a break and have a great lunch
* House of Blues: listen to great Chicago blues

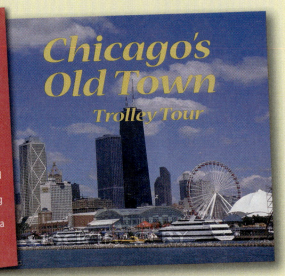

Chicago's Old Town Trolley Tour

Unit 10 On the other hand

4. 🎧 Listen to the model conversation and look at the chart.

5. **PAIRS.** Take turns. Do the ability tests and take notes in the chart.

Test	You	Your partner
wink To wink is to close and open one eye as a signal to someone. Can you?		
wiggle your ears It takes great muscle control to move only your ears. Can you?		
touch your toes without bending your knees Some people are able to touch their toes without bending their knees. Can you?		
whistle a famous song Can you whistle a well-known song? Which one?		

6. **GROUPS OF 4.** Report your results to another pair.

Before   **After**

Unit 11 Trading spaces

7 🎧 Listen to the model conversation and look at the pictures.

8 *PAIRS.* While you were away at school, your mother has completely remodeled the kitchen. Look at the photos and take turns saying what she's done. Talk about these kitchen items.

cabinets	counter top	dishwasher	pots and pans
sink	spice rack	stove	

9 Are you happy with the changes? Why or why not?

Unit 12 A soccer fan's website

10 🎧 Listen to the model conversation.

11 *GROUPS OF 3.* Take turns talking about your weekend plans. Name at least two things you might do each day and two things you might not do.

World of Music 2

My Way
Frank Sinatra

Vocabulary

1 **PAIRS.** Match the expressions with their meanings.

1. He faced the final curtain. _e_
2. He followed a charted course. ___
3. I bit off more than I could chew. ___
4. I saw it through. ___
5. They stood tall. ___

6. He had his fill. ___

7. I took the blows. ___

a. I finished it completely.
b. I took on more than I could handle.
c. I accepted the consequences.
d. He had enough.
e. He met the end without fear.
f. He had a plan for his actions.
g. They were proud and determined.

Listening

2 🎧 Listen to the song. What kind of person does the song portray?

1. regretful and depressed
2. proud and independent
3. adventurous and irresponsible

3 🎧 Listen to the song again and complete the lyrics on page 59.

4 **PAIRS.** Compare your answers.

From the 1940s through the 1980s, **Frank Sinatra** was probably the most famous entertainer in the U.S. Sinatra lived his life without caring what people thought, and the song, "My Way," became his signature song.

My Way

And now, the end is near;

And so I face the final ____.

My friend, I'll say it clear,

I'll state my case, of which I'm certain.

____ ____ a life that's full.

____ ____ each and ev'ry highway;

And more, much more than this,

I ____ ____ my way.

Regrets, ____ ____ a few;

But then again, too few to mention.

I did what I ____ to do

And ____ it through without exemption.

I _____ each charted course;

Each careful step along the byway,

And more, much more than this,

I ____ ____ my way.

Yes, there were times, I'm sure ____ ____

When I ____ ____ more than I ____ chew.

But through it all, when ____ ____ doubt,

I ate it up and spit it out.

____ ____ it all and I ___ tall;

____ ____ ____ my way.

____ ____, ____ laughed and ____.

____ ____ my fill, my share of losing.

And now, as tears subside,

I find it all so amusing.

To think I did all that;

And may I say – "Not in a shy way,"

Oh no, oh no, not me,

I ____ ____ my way.

For what is a man, what has he got?

If not himself, then he has not

to say the things he truly feels,

And not the words of one who kneels.

The record shows I ____ the blows –

____ ____ ____ my way!

Speaking

5 *GROUPS OF 3.* **Discuss these questions.**

What lines from the song best explain the character's personality?
Sinatra announced his retirement two years after recording "My Way."
Do you think the singer is expressing a personal feeling in this song?
Why or why not?

Green card

Vocabulary Immigration
Grammar Review: present perfect with *for* and *since*
Speaking Talking about how long you have done something

Getting started

1 **_PAIRS._** **Complete the text with the words in the box.**

green card	ID (identification) card	immigration	nationalities
passport	permanent resident	~~tourist visa~~	work permit

GOING TO THE UNITED STATES

Before you visit the United States, check to see if you need a (1) _tourist visa_. Some (2) _____ need to have one, but others don't. If you have a valid visa but want to stay longer than 90 days, you can apply to the (3) _____ department for an extension. If you want to work in the U.S., you need a (4) _____. If you want to live and work in the U.S. permanently, you need to go through a long process to get a (5) _____. When you get it, you are considered a (6) _____ of the United States. No matter what your status, it is a good idea to carry an (7) _____ or your (8) _____ with you so that you can prove who you are.

2 🎧 **Listen and check your answers.**

3 **_PAIRS._** **Talk about a trip you'd like to take to another country. Use as many words from Exercise 1 as you can.**

I'd like to go to Spain. First I need to get a passport. I don't need a tourist visa because . . .

Reading

4 Kate and Rod Bolton recently got married. They are from different countries. Why do you think an immigration officer is interviewing them?

5 Read the officer's notes and check your answer.

Case number: 247 – Kate Bolton (English)
Rod Bolton (American)

Reason for interview: Kate Bolton – application for green card. Check that the marriage is a real marriage.

Summary of what Rod Bolton said during his interview:

- Kate came to the U.S. eight months ago, but she lived in San Francisco when she first got here.
- He (Rod Bolton) met Kate at a party in New York six months ago, and they fell in love immediately.
- They were married three months ago.
- Kate is a dance teacher.
- They usually do everything together. They like the same things.

6 Read the officer's notes again and complete the first column of the chart with the information Rod gave him.

	Rod's answers	Kate's answers
1. When did Kate come to the U.S.?	8 months ago	
2. Where did she live before she came to New York?		
3. When did Kate and Rod meet?		
4. Where did they meet?		
5. When did they get married?		
6. What is Kate's job?		
7. Do they like doing the same things?		

7 🎧 Listen to the immigration officer's interview with Kate. Complete the chart in Exercise 6 with Kate's information.

8 *PAIRS.* Look at the information in Exercise 6. What information is different?

Kate said she met Rod four months ago, but Rod said it was six months ago.

Grammar focus

1   **Study the examples of present perfect with *for* and *since*.**

> **(+)** I've known him **for** four months.
> **(–)** She hasn't been to the U.K. **since** last year.
> **(?)** Has she lived in New York **for** a long time?
>   Yes, she has. / No, she hasn't.

2   **Look at the examples again. Underline *for* or *since* to complete the rules in the chart.**

Present perfect with *for* and *since*
Use **for / since** to talk about a period of time.
Use **for / since** to talk about a specific point in time.

> **Grammar Reference page 146**

3   **Write the expressions from the box in the correct columns.**

a couple of days	ages	an hour	Friday	4:00 A.M.	I was a child
last summer	May	nine months	two years	2001	

for	since
a couple of days	Friday

4   **Use the correct form of the verb in parentheses or *for* or *since* to complete the conversation between Rod (R) and the immigration officer (I).**

I: Nice cat. **(1)** _Have you had_ **(you/have)** him **(2)** _____for_____ a long time?

R: Yes, I **(3)** _____ **(have)** him **(4)** _____ ten years.

I: And how long **(5)** _____ **(you/live)** in this apartment, Mr. Bolton?

R: **(6)** _____ April 15.

I: And your wife? How long **(7)** _____ **(she/be)** in the United States?

R: **(8)** _____ last September.

I: And how long **(9)** _____ **(you/know)** your wife?

R: **(10)** _____ six months.

I: And you **(11)** _____ **(be)** married **(12)** _____ February?

R: Yes, we **(13)** _____ .

I: And your wife **(14)** _____ **(not be)** to England **(15)** _____ last September?

R: No, she **(16)** _____ .

Pronunciation

5 🎧 **Listen. Notice the weak and strong pronunciations of *have* and *has*. Notice that the contracted form of *has* is the same as the contracted form of *is*.**

How long *have* you been married?

We**'ve** been married for three months.

How long *has* she been in the U.S.?

She**'s** been here since September.

Has she been to England since then?

No, she **hasn't**. / Yes, she **has**.

Have you known each other for a long time?

No, we **haven't**. / Yes, we **have**.

Your neighbor **hasn't** seen you together.

We **haven't** lived here very long.

6 🎧 **Listen again and repeat.**

7 *PAIRS.* **Practice the conversation in Exercise 4.**

Speaking

8 *2 PAIRS.* **Students A and B, you are a married couple. Prepare for an immigration interview. Look at page 138. Students C and D, you are immigration officers. Prepare your questions for the interview. Look at page 140.**

9 *2 PAIRS.* **Conduct the interviews. Student C, interview Student A. Student D, interview Student B. Interview them on opposite sides of the room so they can't hear each other's answers! Take notes.**

C: How long have you known each other?
A: We've known each other for about 10 months, since last September.

10 *GROUPS OF 4.* **Students A and B, compare your interviews. Did you give the same answers? Students C and D, compare your notes. Do Students A and B have a real marriage? Tell them your conclusion and your reasons for it.**

Writing

11 **Imagine you are the immigration officer who interviewed Kate and Rod. Write a brief report on your findings. Use the present perfect with *for* or *since* and some of the vocabulary from this unit.**

CONVERSATION TO GO

A: How long **have** you **lived** here?
B: Oh, I**'ve** only **lived** here **for** a few days.
A: Really? I**'ve been** here **since** 1780.

What's that noise?

Vocabulary Sounds people make
Grammar Modals: *must, might, can't* for deduction
Speaking Making deductions

Getting started

1 Label the photos with the verbs in the box.

cheer clap cry laugh scream shout whistle yawn

2 🎧 Listen and match the sounds with the photos.

1. _C_   2. ___   3. ___   4. ___

5. ___   6. ___   7. ___   8. ___

3 **PAIRS.** Take turns making the noises in Exercise 1 and saying what your partner is doing.

A: (yawns)
B: You're yawning.

Listening

4 🎧 **Listen to this radio phone-in contest. Who won the contest? Put a check (✓) next to the name(s).**

Maria
Steve

5 🎧 **Listen again and answer the questions.**

1. Which possible places and jobs does Maria mention?
2. What is Maria's final answer?
3. Which four possible jobs does Steve mention?
4. What is Steve's final answer?
5. What is the correct answer?

6 *PAIRS.* **Make a list of the sounds that Maria and Steve heard. How many can you remember?**

A: People talking.
B: Yes, we also heard traffic.

7 🎧 **Listen to the radio phone-in contest again. Write *T* (true) or *F* (false) after each statement. If the statement is false, write the correct information.**

1. Callers have to listen and guess what the people's jobs are.
2. The prize is four tickets to the radio show.
3. Steve hears a volleyball player. Steve wins.

D _____

E _____

F _____

Grammar focus

1 **Study the examples of modals of deduction + *be*.**

> He **might be** a bus driver, but I'm not sure.
> He **must be** a bus driver. Look at his uniform.
> He **can't be** a bus driver. He's too young.

2 **Look at the examples again. Write *must, might,* or *can't* next to the correct description in the chart.**

Modals: *must, might, can't* for deduction
How sure are you?
Almost 100% sure something is true. _____
About 50% sure something is true. _____
Almost 100% sure something is NOT true. _____

> *Grammar Reference page 146*

3 **Complete the conversations with *must be, might be,* or *can't be*.**

1. A: How long was your flight from Singapore?

   B: Twenty-six hours.

   A: Wow! You ___must be___ really tired.

2. A: Who's that woman talking to Won-jin?

   B: Well, she looks a lot like her, so it _____ her sister.

3. A: I can't find my glasses.

   B: They _____ in the bathroom. You leave them there sometimes.

4. A: What's that noise upstairs?

   B: I don't know, but it _____ the cat. She's outside.

5. A: Sam never studies, but he always passes his exams.

   B: Well, they _____ very difficult exams then.

6. A: Listen to his accent. He _____ American.

   B: Not necessarily. He _____ from Canada.

7. A: Linda and Jeff are going to Bermuda again. It's their fourth vacation there this year!

   B: They _____ very wealthy.

8. A: I can't find the scissors.

   B: You just had them a minute ago, so they _____ very far away.

Pronunciation

4 🎧 **Listen. Notice the weak or disappearing sound of the *t* in *might be, can't be,* and *must be.***

He might be at an airport.   He can't be a taxi driver.   He must be a bus driver.

She might be British.   No, she can't be.   Then she must be Australian.

5 🎧 **Listen again and repeat.**

6 *PAIRS.* **Practice the conversations in Exercise 3.**

Speaking

7 🎧 *PAIRS.* **You're going to be in a phone-in contest. Write your answers in the chart under *Game 1*.**

1. Listen to the first clue. What are all the possible jobs? Tell your partner.
2. Listen to the next clue. Are all the jobs possible? Tell your partner why or why not.
3. Listen to the last clue. You should only have one job left.
4. Listen to the complete sequence. What is the job? Were you correct?

	Game 1	Game 2
1st clue: all possible jobs		
2nd clue: likely jobs unlikely jobs		
3rd clue: final guess		
correct answer		

8 🎧 *PAIRS.* **Play again. Listen to another mystery job. Follow the steps from Exercise 7. Record your answers in the chart under *Game 2*.**

Writing

9 **Write about a mystery job of a relative or a friend. Describe what the person does at his or her job, but do not make it obvious.**

CONVERSATION TO GO

A: That **might be** John at the door.
B: No, it **can't be**. He's on vacation—in Brazil.
A: Then it **must be** Peter.

Mumbai Soap

Vocabulary Topics for TV soap operas
Grammar *will/won't* for future
Speaking Predicting the future

Lesson A

Getting started

1 Do you watch soap operas on TV? Which is your favorite one?

2 Which five topics do you most often see in soap operas? Check (✓) the topics in the box.

crime	death	family life	greed	illness
marriage	misfortune	money	power	romance

3 *PAIRS.* Compare your answers.

Reading

4 Look at the photos of scenes from a television soap opera from India. Which topics in Exercise 2 do you think the soap opera is about?

5 Read Part One of the soap opera and check your answers to Exercise 4.

PART ONE

"NINA, you can't leave me," cries Sanjay, and Nina thinks her heart will break. She thinks about the soccer match in Mumbai where she met Sanjay. She knows her parents will never accept this man with no money or family connections. And she loves and respects her parents. They've told her, "Go to London and stay with our family there. You'll soon forget Sanjay."

6 How do you think Nina will solve her problem? Choose *a*, *b*, or *c* and say why.

a. She'll run away and marry Sanjay.
b. She'll stay in India, but she'll stop seeing Sanjay.
c. She'll go to London.

7   Read Part Two of the story and check your predictions.

PART TWO

"WILL we see each other again?" asks Sanjay. "Of course," promises Nina. "And I'll email every day." Her emails tell Sanjay all about her life in London and her acting classes. But they don't mention Ravi, a family friend also living in London. "Marry me, Nina," Ravi says. Nina asks for time to think. The next day she gets a call offering her an important role in a popular British soap opera. When Sanjay finds out about this, he writes, "I know you're happy in London. Please forget me." "No!" cries Nina.

8   What do you think will happen next? Choose *a*, *b*, or *c* and say why.

a. Nina will go back to India and marry Sanjay.
b. She'll accept the job and tell Sanjay about Ravi.
c. She'll accept the job and stay in London.

9   Read Part Three of the story and check your predictions.

PART THREE

FIVE years later, Sanjay turns on the TV in his Liverpool hotel room. Tomorrow he will play soccer for India. He knows Nina is in London, but he doesn't think he'll see her. He still remembers her last email: "I won't marry anyone else, but I must stay in London. It's not just the job . . . it's also my family. I'll always love you." Sanjay can hear her voice. He turns in surprise and sees her on the TV screen. "She's as beautiful as ever. Is it too late?" he asks himself.

15

Grammar focus

1 **Study the examples with** *will* **and** *won't*.

Will for future	*Will* for predictions
(+) I'll (will) always **love** you.	She **thinks** her heart **will break**.
(–) I **won't** (will not) **marry** anyone else.	He **doesn't think** he'll **see** her again.
(?) Will you **remember** me?	**Do** you **think** it **will be** too late?

2 **Look at the examples again. Underline the correct words to complete the explanations in the chart.**

will/won't for future predictions
Use *will* or *won't* to talk about something that you **think / know** is going to happen.
Use *don't think* + subject + *will* to talk about something you think **is / isn't** going happen.

Grammar Reference page 146

3 **Complete the text with** *will* **or** *won't* **and a verb from the box. Use contractions when possible.**

call   get   go   happen   marry   meet   recognize   speak

What do you think **(1)** ___will happen___ in the final episode of "Mumbai Soap"?

I think Sanjay **(2)** _____ Nina's phone number from a mutual friend. He

(3) _____ her, but he'll hear a man's voice and he **(4)** _____ **(not)**.

But Nina and Sanjay **(5)** _____ again. I think Nina **(6)** _____ to

Liverpool to watch the soccer game with friends. I don't think she **(7)** _____

Sanjay at first. But he'll be the hero of the game. Do you think Nina **(8)** _____

Sanjay at last?

Pronunciation

4 🎧 **Listen. Notice the pronunciation of the contracted and weak forms of** *will*.

I'll always	I'll always love you.
you'll forget	You'll forget me.
it'll be	Do you think it'll be too late?
her heart will break	She thinks her heart will break.

5 🎧 **Listen again and repeat.**

Speaking

6 *BEFORE YOU SPEAK.* **What do you think will happen in the final episode of "Mumbai Soap"? Write your notes in the chart.**

I think . . .   I don't think . . .

Nina

Sanjay

Ravi

Nina's Parents

7 *GROUPS OF 4.* **Take turns telling each other how you predict the soap opera will end.**

Family life is very important to Nina, so I think she'll tell her parents about Sanjay. I don't think they'll be happy . . .

8 🎧 **Listen to the summary of the last episode and check your predictions.**

Writing

9 **Write a note to a friend. Make predictions about one of these things. Use *will* or *won't*.**

- What will happen in the next episode of your favorite TV program?
- What will be the result of the next big sports event in your area?
- What will be the main story in tomorrow's newspapers?

CONVERSATION TO GO

A: **Will** you **ever** see her again?
B: No, I **don't think** I **will**.

Lesson A

The message behind the ad

Vocabulary Adjectives used in advertisements
Grammar Future factual conditional (*If* + simple present + *will*)
Speaking Talking about future possibilities

Getting started

1 **Underline the best adjectives to complete the sentences about the products.**

1. Medallion is a **delicious** / **shiny** new coffee. Try it—you'll love it.
2. You'll have **shiny** / **fresh** hair every time you use Gloss shampoo. So, for **reliable** / **healthy-looking** hair, use Gloss today.
3. Sunease sunscreen will keep your skin **fast** / **safe** from sunburn all through the day. And it keeps your skin **delicious** / **soft**, too!
4. Drink **safe** / **fresh** Sundew orange juice for breakfast—the **clean** / **healthy** way to start your day.
5. Now Lux-Clean laundry soap is even better. Your clothes will always be **clean** / **delicious** and very **reliable** / **soft**.
6. If you dream of working with a **soft** / **fast** and totally **healthy** / **reliable** computer, try the new VMC laptop today.

2 **PAIRS.** Compare your answers.

Reading

3 **Read the article about viewers' reactions to television ads. Are their reactions positive or negative?**

Talking Back to Ads

ADS ON TV ARE A ONE-WAY STREET – they talk and we listen. But, does it have to be that way? Last week, we encouraged television viewers to talk back to advertisers about how people in the ads are portrayed. If you believe you can make a difference, read what some people had to say about most TV ads.

Yoko, a college student, said, "Advertisers seem to think that if they show thin, attractive people, everyone will want to buy what they're selling, whether it's a car, a soft drink, or perfume. I like to see ads that have real people in them, not just good-looking models."

Roger, a computer analyst, is especially worried about ads that target young children. "I have an eleven-year-old son, and I don't want him to think that physical appearance is the most important thing in life. A lot of TV ads tell kids that if they don't wear certain clothes, they won't be popular with other kids."

If you call or write to the advertiser and the TV network every time you see an ad that offends you, you will be able to change the way advertisers portray people. Let advertisers know what you think!

4 **Read the article again and answer the questions.**

1. What does the article encourage people to do? Why?
2. What kind of people would Yoko like to see on TV?
3. Why is Roger especially worried about ads that target young children?

Listening

5 **GROUPS OF 3. Describe an advertisement you've seen recently. What was the message of the ad?**

The new ad for Super-Fresh shampoo shows beautiful women having a great time dancing. The message is, "Use this shampoo and you'll be beautiful and happy."

6 🎧 **Listen to the interview with an advertising executive. Check (✓) the photos of the products in Exercise 1 that they talk about.**

7 🎧 **Listen again and answer the questions.**

1. What kind of people do they use in car advertisements?
2. Which products often use families in their advertisements?
3. Why is humor a good thing to use in ads?

Grammar focus

1 **Study the examples of the future real conditional.**

> **(+)** **If** you **buy** this car, you**'ll meet** a beautiful woman.
> People **will remember** the ad **if** it**'s** funny.
> **(–)** **If** you **use** this sunscreen, your kids **won't get** sunburned.
> You **won't** regret it **if** you **try** our product.
> **(?)** What **will happen if** I **buy** this car?

2 **Look at the examples again. Underline the correct word or phrase to complete the rules in the chart.**

> **Future real conditional**
>
> Use the future real conditional to talk about things that may or may not happen.
>
> The verb in the *if* clause is in the **simple present / future**.
>
> When the *if* clause comes first, it **is / isn't** usually followed by a comma (,).

> *Grammar Reference page 146*

3 **Complete the sentences with the correct form of the verbs in parentheses.**

1. You _'ll lose_ (**lose**) weight quickly if you _don't eat_ (**not eat**) sweet things.
2. If you _____ (**try**) this lemonade, you _____ (**not want**) to drink anything else.
3. If you _____ (**use**) Gloss shampoo, your hair _____ (**look**) really shiny.
4. You _____ (**have**) more energy if you _____ (**eat**) lots of fresh fruit.
5. If the machine _____ (**break**), we _____ (**repair**) it free of charge.
6. If you _____ (**drink**) Vita-mint, you _____ (**have**) lots of energy all day long.
7. You _____ (**not feel**) so tired if you _____ (**exercise**) at our gym every day.
8. Your skin _____ (**be**) softer if you _____ (**wash**) with Callon soap every day.

Pronunciation

4 🎧 **Listen. Notice the intonation in these conditional sentences.**

If you buy this car, you'll meet a beautiful woman.

If the ad is funny, people will remember it.

If you use this sunscreen, your kids won't get sunburned.

If you try our product, you won't regret it.

5 🎧 **Listen again and repeat.**

Perfume
for the
woman
on the go

START THE DAY WITH JUICE

Syncron:
Sink into Action

Speaking

6 *BEFORE YOU SPEAK.* **Look at the advertisements above. Who are the advertisers "targeting" (trying to sell the products to)? Make notes.**

- young, middle-aged, or older people?
- men, women, or both?
- single or married people?
- people with children?

7 *PAIRS.* **Discuss each ad. Who are the advertisers targeting? What is the message behind each ad?**

I think they're targeting . . .
To me, the message is, "If you use this . . ."

8 **Report on the messages. Do your classmates agree?**

Writing

9 **You work for an advertising agency. Write a paragraph with ideas for an ad to sell a product you use and like. Use the future real conditional.**

CONVERSATION TO GO

A: If you **buy** this car, you**'ll get** a lot of attention.
B: Especially from my mechanic!

Unit 13 Green card

1 🎧 Listen to the model conversation.

2 *2 PAIRS.* Break into pairs. Students A and B, look at page 139. Students C and D, look at page 140.

3 Students A and C, interview each other. Students B and D, interview each other. Take notes.

4 *GROUPS OF 4.* Students A and B, compare your notes. Students C and D, compare your notes. Are Students A and B really roommates? Are Students C and D? How do you know?

Unit 14 What's that noise?

5 🎧 Listen to the model conversation.

6 *PAIRS.* Write down the name of four places and a few of the sounds you hear in each, for example, *concert: people clapping, people singing.*

7 *2 PAIRS.* Take turns telling the other pair the sounds you wrote down in Exercise 6. Do not say the name of the place. The other pair can have only three guesses. Each guess is one point. Keep score. The pair with the lowest number of points wins the game.

Unit 15 Mumbai Soap

8 *BEFORE YOU SPEAK.* Read the TV guide. What do you think will happen on Wednesday? What do you think will happen on Friday?

TV GUIDE - WEEK IN REVIEW

Final week of
Love Me or Leave Me

MONDAY	TUESDAY	WEDNESDAY	THURSDAY	FRIDAY
Five days before their wedding, Linda and Evan have a huge fight and break up.	Linda visits an old boyfriend in San Francisco, and Evan goes fishing.	Evan an_ make_ are _ th____ _e.	Linda and Evan go to the wedding rehearsal. The radio station BRMB is there to broadcast the wedding and interview them live before and after their wedding.	Tune in for the grand finale – the final episode of "Love Me or Leave Me."

9 🎧 Listen to the model conversation and look at the photos.

10 *PAIRS.* Share your predictions.

Unit 16 The message behind the ad

11 🎧 Listen to the model conversation.

12 *BEFORE YOU SPEAK.* Choose a product and write an advertising slogan using an *if* clause.

13 *GROUPS OF 3.* Share your slogan with two classmates. Who came up with the best slogan? The funniest slogan? The most creative slogan?

UNIT 17 Willpower

Vocabulary Phrasal verbs
Grammar Verbs + gerund; verbs + infinitive
Speaking Talking about changing habits

Lesson A

Getting started

1 *Willpower* is the ability to control your mind and body in order to achieve something. Match the phrasal verbs about willpower with the correct definitions. You will use one definition twice.

Phrasal verbs	Definitions
1. I heard that you **took up** yoga recently. _d_	a. stopped doing something that you did regularly before
2. I can't believe she **threw away** all the chocolates! ___	b. did not accept an offer or opportunity
3. I finally **gave up** drinking coffee in the afternoon. ___	c. continue to do something
4. You'll have to **cut down on** desserts if you want to lose weight. ___	d. started doing a particular activity
5. I **keep on** going to the gym every day, even though I hate it. ___	e. avoid doing something that you should do
6. Every day she has a new excuse to **get out of** exercising. ___	f. put something in the trash
7. Many people **cut back on** carbohydrates to lose weight. ___	g. reduce the amount, number, or size of something
8. I **turned down** their dinner invitation because I'm on a diet. ___	

2 **PAIRS.** Take turns telling each other about something you've begun doing or cut back on recently. Use some of the phrasal verbs in Exercise 1.

Last summer, I took up tennis. I tried to cut down on sweets, but I just couldn't give up ice cream.

3 **PAIRS.** Discuss these questions.

Which of these things take a lot of willpower?
Which don't take much willpower?

• exercising
• giving up drinking coffee
• getting organized
• giving up watching television
• learning to speak a new language
• learning to play a musical instrument

Reading

4 Take the the quiz to find out how much willpower you have.

Do you have willpower?

Can you do things even if they're difficult? Can you finish what you start? Read each situation and circle *a, b,* or *c*.

1 You have stopped eating sweets, but today you're home alone and you're hungry. There's a box of chocolates in the kitchen. Do you decide to:
a. eat all the chocolates but not buy any more?
b. throw away the whole box and give up eating sweets forever?
c. eat one or two and then throw away the rest?

2 You love buying new things, but you already have too much charged on your credit card. You realize you need to cut down on spending. Will you:
a. try to shop only when there are sales?
b. quit shopping until all your bills are paid?
c. only shop when you really need to buy something?

3 You have a bad temper and your family dislikes going places with you. Do you decide to:
a. not worry about how your family feels?
b. take an anger management course and learn to control your temper?

c. practice not losing your temper, but if you do, be sure to apologize?

4 You don't enjoy exercising, but you want to get in shape. You take up jogging. One day as you start jogging, you meet a good friend who invites you for coffee. Will you:
a. stop to have a cup of coffee with your friend?
b. give an excuse to get out of having coffee and keep on jogging?
c. promise to meet him or her in five minutes and only jog around the park once?

5 Count the number of *a*'s, *b*'s, and *c*'s you circled. Then turn to page 137 to find out how much willpower you have.

6 *PAIRS.* Tell your partner your results on the willpower quiz. Do you agree or disagree with the results? Why? What can you do to have more willpower?

Grammar focus

1 Study the examples of verbs followed by gerunds and infinitives.

Verbs + gerund	Verbs + infinitive
(+) He **kept on** running.	I **want to eat** something.
(–) I don't **enjoy doing** exercise.	You **don't need to have** a cup of coffee.
(?) Did you **give up drinking** soda?	Did he **learn to control** his temper?

2 Look at the verbs in the box. Find these verbs in the quiz in Exercise 4. Put them into the correct column in the chart.

decide	give up	cut down on	need	quit
dislike	practice	learn	enjoy	get out of
want	take up	keep on	stop	promise

Verbs followed by gerund	Verbs followed by infinitive
give up	decide

Grammar Reference page 147

3 Complete the paragraph with the correct form of the verbs in parentheses.

Before I went to Mexico on vacation, I decided _____ Spanish classes.
　　　　　　　　　　　　　　　　　　　　　　　　　　1. (take)

I needed _____ work early to get to class. The class was hard, so I quit
　　　　　2. (leave)

_____ it and got some Spanish cassettes. I didn't enjoy _____ to
　　3. (take)　　　　　　　　　　　　　　　　　　　　　　　　4. (listen)

the cassettes, but I didn't want _____ _____ Spanish. I kept on
　　　　　　　　　　　　　　　　5. (give up)　　6. (learn)

_____ to study, but I didn't have enough time. So I finally stopped
　7. (try)

_____ . When I got to Mexico, I found that many people there speak
　8. (try)

some English, and they were happy to practice _____ English with me!
　　　　　　　　　　　　　　　　　　　　　　　　9. (speak)

Pronunciation

4 🎧 Listen. Notice the weak pronunciation of *to* in the verbs followed by infinitives and the disappearing /t/ sound in *want to* ("wanna").

I want to lose weight.

I need to get more exercise.

I learned to play tennis.

But then I wanted to eat more.

I want to eat less.

I decided to stop eating chocolate.

I decided to go jogging every day.

And I needed to lose more weight.

5 🎧 Listen again and repeat.

Speaking

6 *GROUPS OF 3.* Take turns. Toss a coin (one side of the coin = move one space, the other side of the coin = move two spaces). When you land on a space, use the cues to make a sentence. If your sentence is correct, stay on the space. If it is incorrect, move back to where you started your turn. The first person to reach FINISH wins.

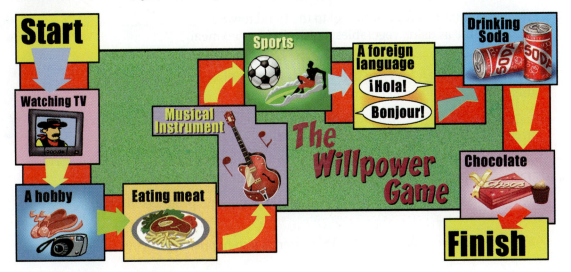

Writing

7 Write a letter to a friend. Describe recent changes you have made either in your work life or personal life, including things you have given up, cut back on, or taken up. You can use your imagination. Use verbs + gerund, verbs + infinitive, and some of the phrasal verbs from this unit.

CONVERSATION TO GO

A: Could I have a piece of your chocolate?

B: Sure. But didn't you **quit eating** chocolate?

A: No. I only **gave up buying** chocolate.

Wave of the future

Vocabulary Words related to new trends
Grammar *Used to* and *would*
Speaking Comparing past and present trends

A

Lesson A

Getting started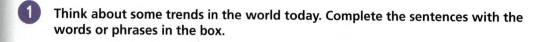

1 Think about some trends in the world today. Complete the sentences with the words or phrases in the box.

alternative medicine	genetic engineering	hybrid cars	instant messaging
renewable resources	telecommuting	vegetarianism	

1. People are looking for ways to use <u>renewable resources</u>, like solar energy or windmills, for their energy needs.

2. _____ is quickly replacing the telephone as an easy way to communicate, especially among teenagers.

3. Many restaurants have responded to the trend toward _____ and serve meals using vegetables and grains, but no meat.

4. Instead of traveling to an office, many people are turning to _____. They use phones, faxes, mail, and the Internet to do their jobs without leaving home.

5. _____ use both gasoline and electricity. They are considered friendly to the environment.

6. Acupuncture, herbal remedies, and other traditional Chinese practices have become popular forms of _____ in the U.S.

7. Scientists use _____ to alter agricultural products like corn.

2 **PAIRS.** Compare your answers. Are these trends also happening in your country?

3 Look at the photos. Which of the trends in Exercise 1 does each one show?

4 **GROUPS OF 3.** Discuss these questions.

What's one advantage and one disadvantage of each trend in Exercise 1?
Which trends do you think will most likely become widespread?
Which trends will die out?

A: *Telecommuting has the advantage that you don't have to waste time getting to and from work.*
B: *I agree, but a disadvantage is that you have no personal contact with your coworkers.*

Listening

5 🎧 **Listen to the first part of the conversation between Beth and Han-su. What's Beth's job?**

6 🎧 **Listen to the second part of the conversation. Write *T* (true) or *F* (false) after each statement.**

According to Beth . . .

1. people used to think that regular books and magazines would disappear. T
2. telecommuting is not very common.
3. people know we need to use renewable resources.
4. people don't worry about wasting energy.
5. solar panels will soon be on every home and business.
6. SUVs are a wave of the future.

7 *PAIRS.* **Compare your answers.**

Grammar focus

1 **Look at the examples. Which of these express a past action?**
Which of these express a past state? Write *PA* or *PS* next to each one.

> **(+)** People **used to** think that regular books would disappear.
>   We **would** get up, get dressed, and go to our work places.
>   My sister **used to** drive a small car. Now she drives an SUV.
>
> **(–)** People **didn't use to** worry about wasting energy.
>   A few years ago, people **wouldn't** stop talking about e-books.
>
> **(?) Did** she **use to** drive a large car?

2 **Look at the examples again. Fill in the blanks with *used to* or *would* to**
complete the rules in the chart.

Used to and *would*
Use both _____ and _____ for repeated past actions.
Use _____ only to talk about a past state (with *be, have, like, hate* . . .).
NOTE: *Would* usually needs a time reference (*every day, when I was a child*). *Used to* is more common at the beginning of a narrative. Use *would* in later sentences, especially to avoid repetition.

> **Grammar Reference page 147**

3 **Make sentences with a similar meaning, using the correct form of *used to*.**

1. When my brother was younger, he worked twelve hours every day.
   When my brother was younger, he used to work twelve hours every day.

2. I hated sports when I was in school, but now I'm a big soccer fan.

3. In the past, my boss drove her car to work every day,
   but now she uses public transportation.

4. Telecommuting was not very popular years ago, but
   now many people work from home.

5. Tania is a vegetarian now. She ate meat at least
   once a day when she was younger.

6. Beto drives a hybrid car now. He had a regular
   car before.

7. When she was younger, Kim went to the beach
   every weekend.

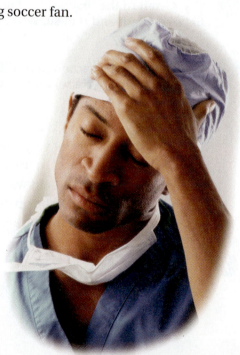

4 **In which sentences from Exercise 3 could you also**
use *would*?

Pronunciation

5 🎧 **Listen. Notice that *used to* and *use to* are pronounced the same way: "use**ta."**

used to	She used to drive a small car.
use to	Did you use to work in an office?
didn't use to	I didn't use to like vegetables.

6 🎧 **Listen again and repeat.**

Speaking

7 *BEFORE YOU SPEAK.* **Think about your past and current habits. Complete the sentences.**

8 *PAIRS.* **Take turns telling each other about your past and present habits. Ask follow-up questions.**

A: I used to eat a lot of chocolate.
B: Really? Would you have chocolate every day?
A: Yes, I would.

9 **Tell the class about one of your partner's habits.**

Writing

10 **Compare your lifestyle with that of your parents when they were your age. What is different? What things were better or worse? Use *used to* and *would*.**

1. Eating habits
   I used to eat a lot of _____.
   I would buy _____ all the time.
   Now I _____
   _____
   _____.

2. Commuting
   I used to go to school/ work by _____
   _____ (form of transportation).
   I would spend _____ (amount
   of time) getting ready and traveling.
   Now I _____
   _____
   _____.

3. Other _____
   I used to _____
   _____
   I would _____
   _____
   _____
   Now _____
   _____
   _____.

CONVERSATION TO GO

A: I **used to** live in the city, but last year we moved to the countryside.
B: I did the opposite. I **used to** have a house in the suburbs, and **I'd** drive two hours to work every day.

Made in the U.S.A.

Vocabulary Materials; possessions
Grammar Passive (simple present)
Speaking Describing where things come from

Getting started

1 Look at the pictures of items you can buy at Fisherman's Wharf in San Francisco. Match each item with the material.

1. cotton __G__   2. glass _____   3. gold _____   4. leather _____

5. pewter _____   6. lycra _____   7. silver _____   8. wood _____

2 🎧 Listen and check your answers. Then listen again and repeat.

3 *PAIRS.* Take turns asking and answering the questions.

What things do you typically buy that are made of wood or glass?

Do you prefer silver or gold jewelry? Why?

Do you prefer cotton or polyester clothing? Why?

What kinds of leather clothes or accessories do you like?

What is your most treasured possession? What material is it made of?

Visit Fisherman's Wharf
with its spectacular view of the bay and handicrafts from all over the world

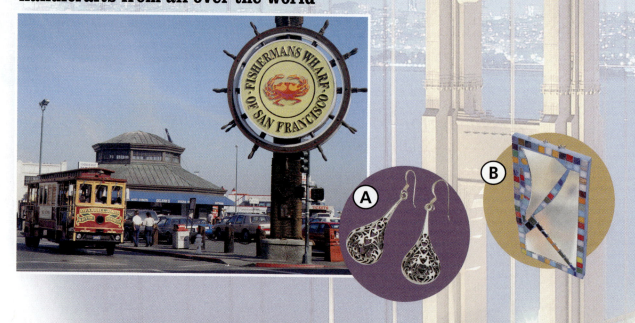

Listening

4 🎧 **Listen to Marcela and Peter, tourists at Fisherman's Wharf in San Francisco. Complete the chart with information on the items they talk about.**

Item	Material	Country of origin	Price
mirror			

5 🎧 **Listen again. Circle the picture of the item Peter buys.**

6 *PAIRS.* **Why does Peter buy it?**

Pronunciation

7 🎧 **Listen. Notice that the sound /n/ or /l/ can form a syllable without a vowel sound.**

cotton   wooden   didn't

metal   sandals   candlesticks

8 🎧 **Listen. Notice how the words with these sounds are pronounced in the sentences.**

They didn't buy the cotton shirt.   They didn't buy the wooden boxes.

They didn't buy the sandals.   They didn't buy the metal candlesticks.

9 🎧 **Listen again and repeat.**

Grammar focus

1 **Study the examples of the active and passive voice.**

Active voice	Passive voice
They make the mirrors in Holland by hand.	The mirrors **are handmade** in Holland.
Artists hand-paint the mirrors.	The mirrors are hand-painted by artists.
The big stores sell it for at least $75.	It's sold in the big stores for at least $75.
Where do they make it?	Where **is** it **made**?

2 **Look at the examples again. Circle *a* or *b* to answer the questions.**

Simple present passive

In the passive sentences, which is more important?

a. the people who make, sell, or buy things   b. the things that they make, sell, or buy

How do you form the simple present passive?

a. *have* + the past participle   b. *be* + the past participle

Grammar Reference page 147

3 **Rewrite the sentences in the passive. Do not mention the agent (the person or thing that does the action) unless it is necessary to understand the sentence.**

1. We call rugs from Turkey, Iran, and Pakistan Oriental rugs.

   Rugs from Turkey, Iran, and Pakistan are called Oriental rugs.

2. Cosmetics companies use fish scales to make lipstick.

3. The U.S. imports most of its electronics from Japan.

4. Both the medical industry and the photography industry use silver.

5. Swiss companies manufacture most of the gold watches in the world.

6. Factories in Canada produce most of the foreign cars sold in the U.S.

7. Food companies add preservatives to food to make it last longer.

8. The supply of materials affects the price of the product.

Speaking

4 Find someone in the class who has something with him or her today, or who is wearing something, made of the materials listed below. Complete the chart with the answers. Find out other details.

A: *Are you wearing anything made of cotton?*
B: *Yes, my jacket is made of cotton.*
A: *Is it handmade?*
B: *No.*
A: *Is it imported?*

Person	Material	Object	Handmade?	Imported?
	cotton			
	gold			
	leather			
	silver			
	wood			

5 **PAIRS.** Take turns telling each other about the results of your survey.

Min-ja's jacket is made of cotton. It's not handmade. It's made in Korea.

6 Take a poll of the class. Find out what things people have that are made of cotton, gold, leather, silver, and wood.

Writing

7 Write a paragraph about something special that you bought on a trip or that someone gave you. Say what it is made of, who made it, and where it was made. Use the passive voice.

CONVERSATION TO GO

A: Did you make that ring?
B: Yes, I did.
A: What's it **made of**?
B: Silver.

UNIT

20 At the movies

Vocabulary Types of movies
Grammar *so, too, neither, (not) either*
Speaking Talking about favorite movies

Lesson A

Getting started

1 Match the comments about movies with the words in the box.

> a) an action movie   b) an animated film   c) a comedy
>
> d) a drama   e) a horror movie   f) a martial arts film   g) a musical
>
> h) a science fiction movie   i) a ~~thriller~~   j) a western

1. It was very intense. The ending was totally surprising. __i__
2. I laughed all the time. _____
3. I loved the music and the dancing. _____
4. It was really scary. I had to close my eyes every five minutes. _____
5. There were lots of fights between cowboys. _____
6. It's set in the future, when computers run the world. _____
7. The hero fought off a whole army with his bare hands. _____
8. It's full of exciting scenes, with lots of explosions and car chases. _____
9. It's a very emotional story about a man who lived alone on an island. _____
10. It's a computer-animated comedy about friendly monsters. _____

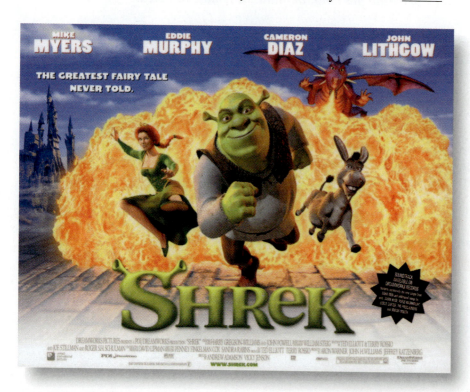

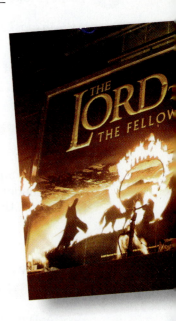

90

Pronunciation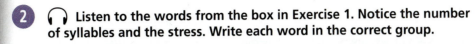

2 🎧 Listen to the words from the box in Exercise 1. Notice the number of syllables and the stress. Write each word in the correct group.

⬤∘	⬤∘∘	∘∘⬤∘	⬤∘∘∘
drama			

3 🎧 Listen and check your answers. Then listen again and repeat.

4 *PAIRS.* Use the words from Exercise 1 to say at least two things about each of the movies in the posters.

Listening

5 *PAIRS.* Guess the answer to each question.

1. Which of these movies made the most money at the box office?
   a. *Star Wars*
   b. *E.T.*
   c. *Titanic*

2. Which of these movies was the most expensive to make?
   a. *Lord of the Rings*
   b. *Star Wars*
   c. *Titanic*

6 🎧 Listen to the interview and check your guesses.

7 🎧 Listen again. Write *T* (true) or *F* (false) after each statement. If the statement is false, write the correct information.

1. The interviewer and the guest both think *Star Wars* is one of the best animated films ever made.

2. Both the interviewer and the guest were surprised at *Titanic's* success.

3. Not many movies have mistakes in them.

4. The most frequent mistake in movies involves the clothes the actors and extras wear.

Grammar focus

1 **Study the examples of additions with *so*, *too*, *neither*, and *not either*.**

> The editors are upset, and **so** are the directors.
> The editors are upset, and the directors are, **too**.
> I didn't know that, and **neither** did the fans.
> I didn't know that, and the fans did**n't either**.

2 **Look at the examples again. Underline the correct information to complete the rules in the chart.**

Additions: *so, too, neither, (not) either*
Additions always use a form of *be*, an auxiliary verb (such as *have* or *do*), or a modal (such as *can, should,* or *will*). The verb tense in the addition must match the verb tense in the first sentence.
Use *so* or *too* if the addition follows **an affirmative / a negative** statement.
Use *neither* or *not either* if the addition follows **an affirmative / a negative** statement.
In additions with *so* and *neither*, the subject comes **after / before** the verb.

> **Grammar Reference page 147**

3 **Rewrite the sentences using *so, too, either,* or *neither*. Remember to use commas correctly.**

1. Both Silvia and Pedro are movie experts.

   Silvia is a movie expert, and so is Pedro.

2. Bruce and David can't go to the movies tonight.

3. Frank and Lois were disappointed in the musical they saw.

4. Russell Crowe and Cameron Diaz are famous actors.

5. Two comedies, *All Day Long* and *Mother*, are playing tonight.

6. Yi-Lian and her friend don't like horror movies.

7. Pat and Omar thought the acting was terrible.

8. Alice and Vera didn't like the ending to the thriller.

4 ***PAIRS.* Compare your answers from Exercise 3. If your answers are the same, what other way could you say the same thing?**

Silvia is a movie expert, and Pedro is, too.

Speaking

5 **GROUPS OF 3.** Take turns asking each other about the kinds of movies you like. What are your favorite movies? Take notes on the survey form.

A: Do you like action movies?
B: Yes. My favorite action movie is The Matrix Reloaded.

Movie Madness				
	Student 1		Student 2	
	like?	favorite	like?	favorite
action movie				
animated film				
comedy				
drama				
horror movie				
martial arts film				
musical				
science fiction				
thriller				
western				

6 Report to the class. Tell what you found out about your classmates' taste in movies.

Senna doesn't like romantic comedies, and neither does Flavia.

Writing

7 Choose two similar movies (for example, two action movies or two comedies). Write a review comparing the two movies. Give some examples from the movies. Use the additions *so*, *too*, *either*, or *neither*.

CONVERSATION TO GO

A: Terry loves action films, and **so does** Alex.
B: Well, I don't like them at all, and **neither does** Dana.

Unit 17 Willpower

1   🎧 Listen to the model conversation.

2   **GROUPS OF 3.** With your group, make up a fictional story. Use at least six verbs from the box plus gerunds or infinitives. Each member of the group contributes at least three sentences to the story.

decide	dislike	enjoy	give up	keep on	learn
need	practice	quit	stop	take up	want

3   Take turns sharing your story with the other groups.

Unit 18 Wave of the future

4   Check (✔) the things your parents used to do in the past. Add two more habits to the list.

Did your parents use to . . .	Name
buy records?	
write long letters to friends and relatives?	
drive a very big car?	
waste electricity?	

5   🎧 Listen to the model conversation.

6   Talk to your classmates. Ask questions until you get "yes" answers to all your questions. Write your classmates' names in the column on the right. Ask follow-up questions.

Unit 19 Made in the U.S.A.

7 **PAIRS.** What are some things you have now that you can try to "sell"? What are they made of? Where are they made? Complete the chart.

Item	Material	Origin
Earrings	Silver and gold	Brazil

8 🎧 Listen to the model conversation.

9 **2 PAIRS.** You and your partner are shopping. Take turns asking the other pair what they are selling, what materials the items are made of, and what countries they come from. Which things would you buy? Switch roles with the other pair.

Unit 20 At the movies

10 🎧 Listen to the model conversation.

11 **GROUPS OF 4.** Write the names of three movies (or TV programs) to talk about. Survey your group members about their opinions. Ask follow-up questions to find out what each person especially likes or dislikes about each movie. Take notes in the chart.

12 Tell the class the results of your survey.

Ron didn't like Endless Night, *and neither did John.*

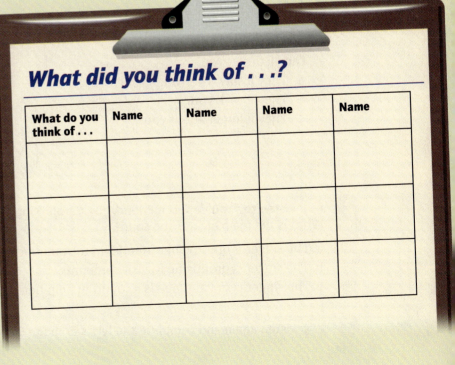

What did you think of . . .?

What do you think of . . .	Name	Name	Name	Name

World of Music 3

You've Got a Friend
Carole King

Vocabulary

1 **GROUPS OF 3.** What do you think these phrases or sentences mean? Choose the best answer.

1. You're down and troubled and need some love and care.
   a. You fell and need help to get up again.
   b. You're sad and in need of a friend.
   c. You don't feel well and need medicine.

2. If the sky above you grows dark
   a. It will get dark soon
   b. If the day gets dark
   c. If things don't go right for you

3. Keep your head together.
   a. Get close to me.
   b. Stay calm.
   c. Avoid an accident.

4. They'll desert you.
   a. They'll stay with you.
   b. They'll trick you.
   c. They'll forget about you.

*Songwriter **Carole King** says that "You've Got a Friend" is one of only two songs that she created through sheer inspiration. The song is a signature tune for singer James Taylor, a long-time friend of King's.*

Listening

2 🎧 Listen to "You've Got a Friend," by Carole King. What is the main idea of the song?

a. The singer is offering her friendship to somebody.
b. The singer is promising to visit someone.
c. The singer is sad and needs a friend to help her.

3 🎧 Listen again and complete the lyrics on page 97.

You've Got a Friend

When you're down and troubled
and you need some love and care
and _____, _____ is going right.
Close your _____ and think of me
and soon I will be there
to brighten up even your _____ night.

You just call out my name,
and you know wherever I am
I'll come running to see you _____.
Winter, spring, summer, or fall,
all you _____ ____ do is call
and I'll be there.
You've got a friend.

If the sky above you
grows dark and full of _____
and that old north ____ begins to blow
Keep your head together and _____
my name out loud
Soon you'll hear me knocking at
your _____.

You just call out my name,
and you know wherever I am
I'll come running, running, yeah, yeah
to see you _____.
Winter, spring, summer, or fall
all you have to do is call
and I'll be there, yes, I will.

Now, ain't it good to know that you've
got a friend
when ____ can be so cold?
They'll _____ you, yes and desert you.
And _____ your soul if you let them.
Ah, but don't you let them.

You just call out my name,
and you know wherever I am
I'll come running, running, yeah, yeah
to see you _____.
_____, spring, _____, or fall,
all you have to do is _____.
And, I'll be there, yes, I will.
You've got a friend.
You've got a friend. Yeah, baby.
You've got a friend.
Ain't it good to know you've got
a friend?
Ain't it good to know you've got
a friend?
Oh, yeah now.
You've got a friend.
Oh yeah.
You've got a friend.

Speaking

4 **GROUPS OF 3.** Discuss these questions. Use lines from the song to explain your answer.

1. When does the singer think a friend is especially useful?
2. How strong are the singer's feelings towards her friend?

How polite are you?

Vocabulary Phrasal verbs with *turn, switch, go*
Grammar Modals: *Could you, Would you, Would you mind* for polite requests
Speaking Making or responding to requests

Getting started

1 **Complete the sentences with the word or words in the box. You will use some words more than once.**

down	~~off~~	on	up	over to

1. I hate it when my alarm goes ___off___ in the morning.

2. That music is too loud. Could you turn it _____, please?

3. Can you turn _____ the lights? I can't see what I'm reading.

4. Please turn _____ all cell phones in the aircraft now.

5. I love that song. Can you turn _____ the volume, please?

6. Would you mind switching _____ Channel 13? I want to watch that Japanese movie.

2 *PAIRS.* **Compare your answers.**

3 *PAIRS.* **Talk about the things you usually turn on when you get home at night. Think about your TV, computer, lights, etc. What do you turn on first, second, and so on?**

When I get home, the first thing I turn on is the lights. Then I always . . .

Reading

4 🎧 Listen to some noises and say what they are. How do you feel about them?

5 **PAIRS.** Discuss these questions. Are you a noisy person? If so, when? Do you feel comfortable asking people to stop making noise?

6 Read the situations in "Excuse me . . ." Circle your answers to the questions.

7 **PAIRS.** Discuss your answers. Which answers are most polite? Which are rude?

"Excuse me . . ."

1 **You're on a bus. The person next to you is playing loud music. What do you say?**

A "Would you mind turning your music down, please?"
B "Driver! Can you tell this guy that it's illegal to play music on the bus?"
C "You're being very rude."

2 **You're on a train. The passenger behind you is kicking your seat. What do you say?**

A "Could you stop doing that, please? I can't concentrate."
B "Conductor! He's kicking my chair!"
C "Stop that now!"

3 **It's the middle of the night. Your neighbor's dog is barking. You can't sleep. You . . .**

A call your neighbor and say, "Could you make Mitzy stop barking, please?"
B call the police and say, "Would you come quickly, there's a dangerous animal next door!"
C open the window and shout, "Be quiet!"

4 **You're having a romantic dinner in a restaurant. A man near you is speaking loudly on his cell phone. What do you say?**

A "Would you mind lowering your voice, please?"
B "Waiter! Please tell this man to go outside."
C "We're trying to have a nice, quiet dinner, and you're disturbing us."

Grammar focus

1 **Study the examples of polite requests and responses.**

Would you please turn the music down?	Of course.
Could I **turn** on the TV?	Sure.
Would you **mind lowering** your voice?	No, of course not.
	Not at all.

2 **Look at the examples again. Underline the correct words to complete the rules in the chart.**

Could you / Would you / Would you mind for polite requests

Use *would you* or *could you* + **the gerund / the base form of the verb** to make polite requests.

Use *Would you mind* + **the gerund / the base form of the verb** to make polite requests.

If you answer *No* to a *would you mind* question, you are saying that you **will / won't** do what the person requests.

Grammar Reference page 148

3 **Look at the pictures. Write polite requests and responses for each situation.**

1. <u>A: Would you mind making</u>
   <u>less noise, please?</u>
   <u>B: No, of course not.</u>

2. _____
   _____
   _____

3. _____
   _____
   _____

4. _____
   _____
   _____

5. _____
   _____
   _____

Pronunciation

4 🎧 **Listen. Notice the way the words** *would you* **and** *could you* **are linked and blended together: "wouldja" and "couldja."**

Would you   Would you please turn the music down?

Would you mind lowering your voice?

Could you   Could you please stop doing that?

Could you make your dog stop barking?

5 🎧 **Listen again and repeat.**

6 *PAIRS.* **Practice the conversations you wrote in Exercise 3.**

Speaking

7 *PAIRS.* **Role-play situations using polite requests. Student A, look at this page. Student B, look at page 142.**

Role-play #1
You left your wallet at home, and you need to borrow money for lunch from Student B, a close friend.

Role-play #2
Student B is your co-worker. Listen and reply.

Role-play #3
You need to stay at home to take care of your sick child. Ask your boss, Student B, for permission to work from home. You will turn on your cell phone so people can call you from work.

Role-play #4
Student B is your neighbor. Listen and reply.

Writing

8 **Look at the quiz in Exercise 6 on page 99. Have you ever been in a situation like any of those? Describe what happened and include the conversation you had with the annoying person.**

CONVERSATION TO GO

A: **Could you turn** your music **down**?
B: What did you say?
A: **Would you mind turning** it **down**?
B: **No, of course not.**

UNIT

22

The art of crime

Vocabulary Words related to crime
Grammar Passive (simple past)
Speaking Describing a crime

Lesson A

Getting started

1 Look at the words associated with crime. Complete the chart.

Crime	Criminal	Verb (+ someone or something)	Meaning
robbery	robber		take money or property illegally from a person or place
burglary		burglarize (a place)	enter a building illegally and take money or goods
mugging	mugger		attack and take something from a person
scam	con artist		use a dishonest plan to get money from somebody
shoplifting		shoplift (something)	take goods from a store without paying
theft		steal (something)	take something illegally

2 🎧 Listen and check your answers. Then listen again and repeat.

3 *PAIRS.* Rank the crimes in Exercise 1 in order of seriousness (1 = the most serious, 6 = the least serious).

4 *GROUPS OF 4.* Decide what punishment each type of criminal deserves.

Should the criminal:
- go to prison? (say for how long)
- pay a fine? (say how much)
- do community service?
  (say what kind of service)

*A: A bank robber should go
to prison for thirty years.*
*B: Thirty years is too much,
especially if no one got hurt.*

Listening

5 **PAIRS.** Look at the painting and read the questions. How much do you know about this painting? Discuss your answers with your partner.

1. It's called the Mona Lisa in English. Do you know what it's called in your language?

2. Who painted it?

3. What happens if you look at the woman's eyes from different angles?

6 🎧 In 1911, the Mona Lisa disappeared. Listen to the story and match the questions with the answers.

1. Who had the idea for the theft? __   a. Eduardo de Valfierno

2. Who stole the painting? __   b. rich collectors

3. Who believed the copies were real? __ c. Vincenzo Perugia

7 🎧 Listen again. Write *T* (true) or *F* (false) after each statement. Correct the false statements.

1. The Mona Lisa was painted by Michelangelo. **F**

   The Mona Lisa was painted by Leonardo Da Vinci.

2. The painting was never found.

3. None of the thieves was ever arrested.

4. Six copies of the painting were made.

Grammar focus

1 Study the examples of active and passive sentences and questions.

Active sentences			Passive sentences		
Subject	**Verb**	**Object**	**Subject**	**Verb**	**Agent**
Da Vinci	painted	the Mona Lisa.	The Mona Lisa	**was painted by**	Da Vinci.
Someone	stole	the painting.	The thieves	**were caught**.	
The police	caught	the thieves.	The painting	**was stolen**.	

Passive questions			
Question word	**Auxiliary**	**Subject**	**Past participle (by)**
Who	**was**	the Mona Lisa	**painted by**?
When	**was**	the painting	**stolen**?
How	**were**	the thieves	**caught**?

2 Look at the examples again. Underline the correct information to complete the explanation in the chart.

Simple past passive
Use the **passive / active** when the action is more important than the person or thing that did the action.

> *Grammar Reference page 148*

3 Rewrite the sentences in the passive. Do not mention the agent (the person or thing that did the action) unless it is important or necessary to understand the sentence.

1. They took over $150,000 from the bank.
   Over $150,000 was taken from the bank.

2. Somebody broke into our house last month.

3. Security personnel arrested many shoplifters during the holiday season.

4. They stole my car yesterday.

5. According to legend, con artists sold the Eiffel Tower dozens of times.

6. The police discovered thousands of pirated CDs.

7. People made copies of the movie months before it reached the video stores.

8. Eduardo de Valfierno sold the Mona Lisa six times.

Pronunciation

4 🎧 Listen to the rhythm in these sentences. Notice that the stressed syllable of each important word is long and clear and that unstressed syllables and unimportant words are short and weak.

How were the **thieves caught**?

Copies of the **paint**ing were **made**.

The o**rig**inal was **off**ered to a **deal**er.

When was the **paint**ing **sto**len?

The **cop**ies were **sold** to coll**ect**ors.

The **paint**ing was re**turned** to the museum.

5 🎧 Listen again and repeat.

Speaking

6 *PAIRS.* You're going to read parts of an article about a famous robbery. Student A, look at page 140. Student B, look at page 142. Read the article. Ask and answer questions about the missing information in your article.

7 Tell the story (without looking at pages 140 and 142) of the Great Train Robbery.

The Great Train Robbery

Writing

8 Write a short newspaper article about a real or imaginary crime that happened recently. Use the passive voice. Include:

- the type of crime
- where/when it happened
- who it happened to
- whether or not the criminal was arrested

CONVERSATION TO GO

A: When **was** your car **stolen**?
B: Last year. The thieves **were** never **caught**.

UNIT 23

A balanced life

Vocabulary Expressions with take
Grammar Review verbs for likes/dislikes followed by gerund and/or infinitive
Speaking Discussing work and after-work activities

Getting started

1 **Look at the pictures and read the conversations. Write the expressions with *take* next to the correct definitions in the chart.**

Expression with *take*	Definition
1. take part in	participate in an activity
2.	agree to do something
3.	relax
4.	begin something new
5.	arrange to have time away from work
6.	stop and have a rest

Peter didn't come in today. He took the day off, and I promised Liz I would do all this work.

Well, I don't mind helping if you've taken on too much work.

I want to get into really good shape so I can take part in the marathon this fall.

Long-distance running is too intense for me. But I've taken up yoga. I really like it!

I can't stand studying anymore. I'm going to watch TV and take it easy for a while.

I need to take a break, too. I'm sick of working on this report.

2 *PAIRS.* Compare your answers.

3 *PAIRS.* Talk about something you want to *take part in*, something you want to *take up*, or something you want to *take a break from*. Ask and answer follow-up questions.

A: *I want to take up karate.*
B: *Are you sure? It requires a lot of dedication.*

Listening

4 *PAIRS.* Look at the photo of Marta and Ian and discuss these questions.

What is happening in the photo?
What are they saying to each other?

5 🎧 Listen to the conversation and answer the questions.

1. What reason does Ian give for not going to the gym?

2. How does Marta react?

3. What is Ian's real reason for not going?

Grammar focus

1 **Study the examples of verbs to express likes and dislikes.**

> Marta **likes to go** to the gym, but Ian **likes watching** basketball on TV.
> Marta **hates watching** sports on TV, but she **loves to work out**.
> He **can't stand working out**, so he **doesn't mind staying** in tonight.
> I **love watching** basketball, but I **hate to watch** the games alone.
> Ian **doesn't enjoy exercising**. He **can't stand to go** to the gym.
> She**'s sick of running**. She**'s into doing** yoga now.

2 **Look at the examples again. Complete the rules in the chart.**

Verbs for likes/dislikes followed by gerunds and/or infinitives
Use the gerund or infinitive after the following verbs: _____, _____, _____, and _____.
Use only the gerund after the following verbs and phrasal verbs: _____, _____, _____, and _____.

Grammar Reference page 148

3 **Write sentences using the prompts. Make any necessary changes. Sometimes more than one correct answer is possible.**

1. I really / can't stand / exercise

   I really can't stand exercising.

2. I / sick of / be out of shape, / so I / decided to / take up jogging

3. Now that it's light out / at 6:00 A.M., / I / not mind / get up early

4. You / really into/ practice / yoga now?

5. I / enjoy / play tennis, / but after an hour / I / like / take / a break

6. Kate's boyfriend / not like / go / to the gym

Pronunciation

4 🎧 **Listen. Notice the groups of consonant sounds.**

I ca**n't st**and **pl**aying tennis, but I do**n't** mi**nd sw**imming.

She ha**tes** watching **sports**, but she lo**ves pract**icing yoga.

He li**kes** e**x**ercising, but sometimes he nee**ds** to take a **br**eak.

5 🎧 **Listen again and repeat.**

Speaking

6 **BEFORE YOU SPEAK.** What are you willing to do to be physically fit?
Check (✔) the things that you are willing to do. Add two more ideas of your own.

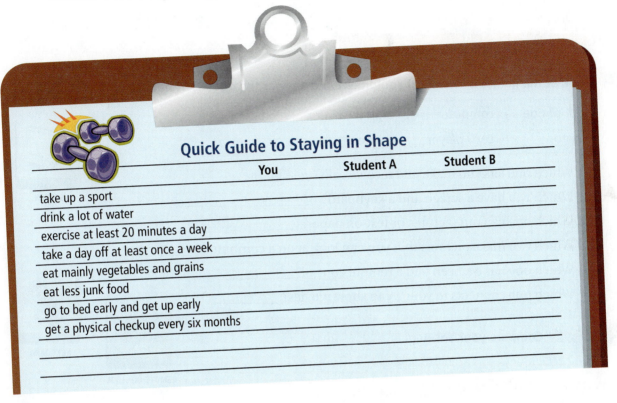

Quick Guide to Staying in Shape

	You	Student A	Student B
take up a sport			
drink a lot of water			
exercise at least 20 minutes a day			
take a day off at least once a week			
eat mainly vegetables and grains			
eat less junk food			
go to bed early and get up early			
get a physical checkup every six months			

7 **GROUPS OF 3.** Take a survey. Take turns asking one another what you are
willing to do. Take notes on the other students' answers.

A: *Would you take up a sport?*
B: *Yes, why not? I like to play soccer, so I don't mind going to the park on
weekends and kicking the ball for a while.*
C: *I really like sports, but I just don't have time right now.*

Writing

8 Write an email to your friend describing how successful (or unsuccessful) you
have been at balancing work and play. Use expressions with *take* and verbs
for likes and dislikes.

CONVERSATION TO GO

A: I **don't mind working** late once in a while, but I **can't stand working**
late every night.
B: Actually, I **like to work** overtime because I **love getting** more money!

Digital age

Vocabulary   Technical equipment
Grammar   Relative clauses with *that, which, who, where*
Speaking   Describing people, places, and things

Getting started

1   **Look at the names of technical equipment and answer the questions below.**

cell phone	computer	digital camera	digital TV
laptop	DVD player	printer	scanner

1. Which one lets you make and receive calls? _cell phone_
2. Which two have a screen and a keyboard? _____ _____
3. Which one can put pictures or text on paper? _____
4. Which two make pictures that you can look at on a computer? _____ _____
5. Which one has a screen and a remote control? _____
6. Which one connects to your TV to show movies? _____

SCREEN

2   ***PAIRS.* Compare your answers.**

Pronunciation

3   🎧 **Listen. Notice the stress. Some of the words in Exercise 1 have two strong syllables.**

keyboard   digital camera

REMOTE CONTROL   **KEYBOARD**

4   ***PAIRS.* Draw a circle over the strong syllable(s) in each word or phrase. The number (2), indicates that there are two strong syllables.**

cell phone	computer	digital TV (2)	DVD player
laptop	printer	remote control (2)	scanner

5   🎧 **Listen and check your answers. Then listen and repeat.**

6   ***GROUPS OF 3.* Discuss these questions.**

Which of the technical equipment in Exercise 1 do you have?
Which would you like to have?
Which do you think is the most useful?

Reading

7 *PAIRS.* **TVs today are different from the first TVs. Can you describe some differences?**

8 **Read the article about digital television. Write *T* (true) or *F* (false) after each statement.**

1. We can communicate with digital TVs. T
2. Traditional TV pictures use more space than digital pictures.
3. Traditional television images can be compressed.
4. Digital pictures of buildings are sent many times.
5. You can receive digital TV anywhere you are.

9 *PAIRS.* **Read the article again and answer the questions.**

1. What is one thing that we can't do with traditional TV that we can do with digital TV?

2. Why can digital systems send and receive more information?

3. What equipment do you need to get digital TV?

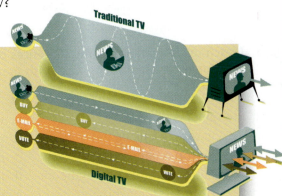

What is digital TV?

In the past, we usually just watched TV. But digital TV is interactive. With digital TV we can easily order things from advertisers, answer quiz questions, or vote on our favorite programs using the remote control. In places where digital TV is very advanced, viewers can get a service that lets them watch any program, when they want to.

So they send a picture of a building once, because it doesn't move. But they send a lot of pictures of people who are walking or cars that are moving around that building.

DO I NEED A SPECIAL TV?
In areas where the service is available, you need either a special TV or a special box that can put the pictures together for your nondigital TV. Then you can watch your favorite program and even "talk" to the station.

HOW DOES DIGITAL TV WORK?
As you know, a TV studio is a place where they produce TV programs. These programs are "the information" sent from the TV studio to our homes. Traditional TV needs a lot of space to send the information.

With digital systems, the information is in digital form and it can be compressed, so the system can send and receive more information.

Additionally, digital TV systems only send the parts of the picture that change.

Grammar focus

1   **Study the examples of relative clauses.**

> They send a lot of pictures of people **who** are walking.
> They send a lot of pictures of people **that** are walking.
> They only send the parts of the picture **that** change.
> They only send the parts of the picture **which** change.
> A television studio is a place **where** they make programs.

2   **Look at the examples again. Complete the rules in the chart with *that*, *which*, *who*, or *where*.**

Relative clauses with *that*, *which*, *who*, and *where*
To introduce relative clauses, use:
_____ for places.
_____ or _____ for things.
_____ or _____ for people.

> *Grammar Reference page 148*

3   **Match the beginnings of the sentences on the left with the endings on the right. Then make complete sentences with *that*, *which*, *who*, or *where*.**

A pilot is someone who flies planes.

1. ~~A pilot is someone~~
2. A garage is a place
3. A laptop is something
4. A computer analyst is someone
5. A printer is a machine
6. A bank is a place
7. A scanner is something
8. A photographer is a person

a. writes computer programs.
b. takes pictures.
c. ~~flies planes.~~
d. puts words and pictures on paper.
e. transfers information into a computer.
f. you can carry around easily.
g. you park your car.
h. you can get money.

Speaking

4 *GROUPS OF 3.* Play the Definitions Game. Take turns reading your definitions. Who can guess the word?

Student A, look at page 138. Student B, look at page 141. Student C, look at page 142.

A: A person who flies planes is . . .
B: A pilot.
A: Correct. You get a point.

Writing

5 Think about all the technical equipment for work or entertainment that you'd like to have. (It could be something that doesn't exist yet, and the cost is not important.) Write a paragraph describing each piece of equipment. Use relative clauses and some of the vocabulary from this unit.

CONVERSATION TO GO

A: I want a digital camera **that's** easy to use.
B: I know a place **where** you can buy a really good one.

Unit 21 How polite are you?

1 🎧 Listen to the model conversation.

2 *PAIRS.* Role-play some situations with requests. Student A, use the information below. Student B, look at page 136.

Student A

Role-play #1
You are a teacher. Student B is your student. You are explaining a difficult math problem, but your student doesn't understand.

Role-play #2
You are riding on a bus. Student B gets on and asks you something.

Role-play #3
You are trying to enjoy a quiet evening in your apartment. Student B is your neighbor, and he or she has the music turned up very loud. Ask your neighbor to turn it down.

Unit 22 The art of crime

3 Read the crime story. Complete the sentences to make your own article. Use your imagination to make the article interesting.

Last night, **(1)** _____ was broken into, and

(2) _____ was stolen. **(3)** _____ and

(4) _____ were attacked by the thief and another

person. Police suspect that the stolen goods were placed

in a **(5)** _____ and taken to **(6)** _____.

Some observers think the crime was an inside job.

4 🎧 Listen to the model conversation.

5 *PAIRS.* Ask questions to find out what your partner's crime story is. Then answer his or her questions about your story.

Unit 23 A balanced life

6 🎧 Listen to the model conversation.

7 *PAIRS.* Ask and answer questions about each other's work and leisure activities.

8 *GROUPS OF 4.* Tell the other pair about your partner's life.

Sylvie has a balanced life. She is really into her job and enjoys going to work every day.
She doesn't mind her boss, except when he's in a bad mood . . .

Unit 24 Digital age

9 Think of five items or occupations and write short definitions for them.
Palm Pilot: thing where you can keep your schedule and all your addresses

10 🎧 Listen to the model conversation.

11 *GROUPS OF 3.* Take turns reading your definitions aloud and guessing the answers.
The first person to guess each item gets 1 point.

Arranged marriages

Vocabulary Wedding party; expressions with *get*
Grammar *It's* + adjective / noun + infinitive to express opinion
Speaking Talking about relationships

Lesson A

Getting started

1 Look at the photo of the wedding party. Identify the people.

bride _D_   best man ___   bridesmaids ___

groom ___   groomsmen ___   maid of honor ___

2 Complete the story with the expressions in the boxes.

~~got engaged~~	get on each other's nerves	got to know

1. Carla and Greg _got engaged_ three years ago. During that time, they
_____ each other very well! Carla and Greg _____ at
times, but most of the time they have a great time together.

get along	got married	gotten over

2. Carla and Greg _____ yesterday. The wedding ceremony was
fine, but there was some tension during the reception. Phil, the best
man, is Greg's best friend. Jenny, Carla's sister, was the maid of honor.
Jenny and Phil went out together for a year. Jenny has never
_____ Phil, and she doesn't _____ with Phil's new
girlfriend.

get back with	get divorced	got upset

3. At some point during the reception, Jenny told Carla that she would
like to _____ Phil. Phil's new girlfriend overheard the
conversation and _____. Carla and Greg started arguing
about Jenny. People thought they were going to _____
before their honeymoon. After a few minutes, everyone calmed
down. Phil told Greg that he was very sorry about the situation.

3 *PAIRS.* Compare your answers.

4 *GROUPS OF 3.* Tell each other about a wedding you've been
to recently.

Pronunciation

5 🎧 **Listen. Notice the different pronunciations of *t* at the end of a word when it links to another *t* and when it links two vowel sounds.**

went out together   They went out together for three years.

during that time   During that time, they got to know each other well.

get upset   At times, they get upset with each other.

get on each other's nerves   Sometimes they get on each other's nerves.

get along well   But most of the time, they get along well.

6 🎧 **Listen again and repeat.**

Listening

7 *PAIRS.* **What is an arranged marriage? Are they now or were they once common in your country?**

8 🎧 **Listen to Monica and Carlos talk about the movie *Monsoon Wedding.* What does Carlos think of arranged marriages?**

9 🎧 **Listen again. Write *T* (true) or *F* (false) after each statement.**

1. In the movie, Aditi's parents want her to marry a man who works in Texas.

2. It's not important for Aditi to marry someone her parents like.

3. Monica thinks that Carlos and his fiancée should see the movie.

4. Carlos will probably go to see *Monsoon Wedding* with his fiancée.

Grammar focus

1 **Study the examples. Notice the ways to express an opinion.**

> It's **important to know** the person you're marrying.
> It's **important for her to marry someone** her parents like.
> It's **a good idea to let** your parents arrange things.
> It's not **a good idea for her to marry** a stranger.

2 **Look at the examples again. Underline the correct information to complete the rules in the chart.**

> **It's + adjective/noun to express opinion**
>
> *It's* can be followed by an adjective or a noun **+ infinitive / gerund.**
>
> Use *for* + **subject / object** before the infinitive when you want to specify *who*.

> **Grammar Reference page 148**

3 **Use the words in columns 1 and 3 to write eight logical sentences. Begin each sentence with *It's*. Make some sentences with the words in column 2 to specify *who*.**

It's a bad idea for someone to get married just to please his or her parents.

1	2	3
		get married just to please his or her parents
(not) important		be engaged for three years before getting married
(not) a good idea	someone	get married without getting engaged first
(not) a bad idea	couples	get to know each other well before getting married
(not) crazy	parents	choose children's marriage partners
(not) absurd	people	try to get along with each other's parents
(not) wonderful		marry someone with similar interests
		maintain some independence

4 *PAIRS.* **Compare your sentences.**

Speaking

5 *BEFORE YOU SPEAK.* Read the advice in the guide and add two more statements.

The Complete Guide for Couples

♥ You should let your parents help you choose your spouse.

♥ Couples should stay close to their families after getting married.

♥ You should choose someone you have known for a long time.

♥ Both spouses should develop and maintain their own interests.

♥ You should share all your problems with your spouse. Don't keep anything to yourself.

♥ Couples should enjoy doing the same kinds of things.

♥ _____
_____

♥ _____
_____

6 *PAIRS.* Share your opinions about each statement.

A: I think it's crazy to let your parents help you choose your spouse.

B: Well, I think it's OK to listen to their opinion, but you have to make the final decision, that's for sure.

7 Take a class poll. Are there any statements most people agree with?

Writing

8 Imagine that you write an advice column for a local newspaper. Today you received this email from a reader. Write your answer. Use *It's* + adjective or noun + infinitive.

To: Vanessa@timesadvice.com
Subject: need help!

I've been married for three years. I would say that, for the most part, my wife and I have had a happy relationship. But now we don't get along very well. She gets upset when I go out with my friends. And on Sundays, I like to watch soccer games. She wants me to go shopping with her, or to visit relatives, but that's really boring. I really love my wife, but I also need some independence. What should I do?

Yours,
Confused

CONVERSATION TO GO

A: I think **it's fine for you** to disagree with me all the time.
B: Oh, you're so wrong. I hardly ever argue with you.

119

Money matters

Vocabulary Money and banks
Grammar Verbs with two objects
Speaking Talking about money

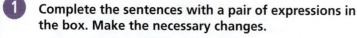

Lesson A

Getting started

1 Complete the sentences with a pair of expressions in the box. Make the necessary changes.

be in the red / be in the black	borrow money / lend money
invest money / save money	bank statement / bank account
checking account / savings account	deposit money / withdraw money
receive interest / pay interest	

1. When you owe money, you <u>are in the red</u>, but once you pay it all back, you <u>are in the black</u> again.

2. You _____ when you put it in the bank, and you _____ if you need it to buy something.

3. People usually keep money for paying bills in a _____ but put their savings in a _____, so that the bank pays them some interest.

4. Banks usually send their customers a _____ every month explaining the activity in their _____.

5. People _____ on the money they have in the bank, but they _____ on money they borrow from the bank.

6. You _____ when you buy something (or shares in a company) to make a profit, and you _____ when you keep it and don't spend it.

7. You _____ from a bank (or someone) when you need more than you have. The bank (or someone) _____ to you.

2 **PAIRS.** Compare your answers.

3 Look at the bank statement and answer the questions.

1. How much money did the customer deposit?

2. How much money did the customer pay in checks?

3. Did the customer pay or receive interest? How much?

4. Is the customer in the black or in the red?

● DirBanking

Statement of account

Checking account number: 81033917

Date		Credits	Debits	Balance
				2,312.78
08/24	Balance brought forward		17.50	2,295.28
08/29	Check #1075		150.00	2,145.28
09/06	Check #1076	500.00		2,645.28
09/15	Electronic Deposit	14.52		2,659.80
09/21	Interest			2,659.80
09/22	Balance brought forward			

4 **PAIRS.** Which of the things in Exercise 1 do you do the most?

Reading

5 *PAIRS.* **Look at the photos showing different ways of banking. Discuss these questions.**

What do you use banks for?

Which of the methods of banking in the pictures do you prefer? Why?

6 **Read the web page for DirBanking. What are three advantages of banking with this online service?**

7 **Read the web page again and answer the questions.**

1. How does DirBanking save you time?

2. Why would you want to borrow money from this bank?

3. How can you access your account?

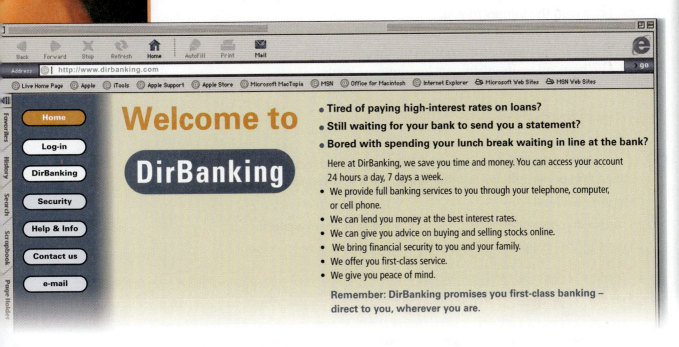

| Home | **Welcome to** | • **Tired of paying high-interest rates on loans?** |

DirBanking

• **Tired of paying high-interest rates on loans?**
• **Still waiting for your bank to send you a statement?**
• **Bored with spending your lunch break waiting in line at the bank?**

Here at DirBanking, we save you time and money. You can access your account 24 hours a day, 7 days a week.
• We provide full banking services to you through your telephone, computer, or cell phone.
• We can lend you money at the best interest rates.
• We can give you advice on buying and selling stocks online.
• We bring financial security to you and your family.
• We offer you first-class service.
• We give you peace of mind.

Remember: DirBanking promises you first-class banking – direct to you, wherever you are.

Home / Log-in / DirBanking / Security / Help & Info / Contact us / e-mail

Grammar focus

1 **Look at the examples with direct and indirect objects. Underline the direct object and circle the indirect object in each sentence.**

> We can lend **you money**.
> We can lend **money to you**.
>
> We bring **your family financial security**.
> We bring **financial security to your family**.

2 **Look at the examples again. Underline the correct words to complete the rules in the chart.**

Verbs with two objects
When the indirect object comes **before** the direct object, **use / do not use** a preposition.
When the indirect object comes **after** the direct object, **use / do not use** a preposition (usually *to* or *for*).

> **Grammar Reference page 149**

3 **Rewrite each sentence by changing the order of the direct and indirect object.**

1. I lent my sister ten dollars.
   I lent ten dollars to my sister.
2. I showed the bank statement to my accountant.
3. Can you send me the bill?
4. She teaches money management to high school students.
5. I can lend the money to you.
6. When will you send me the receipt?
7. Many companies give the option of direct deposit to their employees.
8. The bank offers its customers low-interest loans.

Pronunciation

4 🎧 **Listen. Notice the weak pronunciation of the object pronouns. When *him* or *her* follows another word, the *h* is often silent.**

He sent me a bill.

I can lend you some money.

I gave him a receipt.

They owe us money.

We sent them a check.

Did you buy her a present?

5 🎧 **Listen again and repeat.**

6 🎧 **Complete the sentences with the word you hear: *her*, *him*, or *them*.**

1. I showed _____ the statement.
2. We owe _____ money.
3. I gave _____ a check.
4. Did you give _____ a receipt?
5. I sent _____ a bill.
6. I lent _____ five dollars.

Speaking

7 **BEFORE YOU SPEAK.**
Congratulations! You have won first prize in a contest—$100,000! Now you have to decide what to do with the prize money. Make a list. Be very specific. Use these ideas or other ideas of your own.

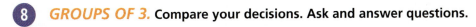

- buy presents for your friends (Who? What presents?)
- keep some for yourself (How much? Invest it?)
- lend some to a friend to start a business (How much? Receive interest?)
- give some to your family (How much?)
- give some to a charity (Which charity? How much?)

8 **GROUPS OF 3.** Compare your decisions. Ask and answer questions.

A: First, I'm going to buy my younger brother a sports car. That will cost about $40,000.
B: Wow! That's generous.
C: Why are you going to do that?

Writing

9 You are the head of an organization that gives money to important social, community, and educational programs in your city or town. Write a letter to a rich, local business owner, explaining how you would distribute one million dollars of his or her money. Use verbs with two objects. Be as specific as you can.

CONVERSATION TO GO

A: Can you lend **me ten dollars**?
B: Sorry, I never lend **money to friends**!

UNIT 27

Less is more

Vocabulary *Waste, use, spend, save* + noun
Grammar Review and expansion: *should/shouldn't, could,*
ought to for advice
Speaking Giving advice

Lesson A

Getting started

1 Look at the word web. It shows how the verb *waste* can go with these nouns.

electricity / energy — paper — time

money — **waste** — opportunities

space — resources

2 **PAIRS.** Make word webs for the verbs *use*, *spend*, and *save*. Use the same nouns as in Exercise 1.

Use

Spend

Save

3 🎧 Listen and check your answers.

4 **PAIRS.** Look at the picture of the office. Make as many sentences as possible using the verb + noun combinations from Exercise 1.

A: *They are wasting electricity because all the lights are on.*
B: *And I'm sure they also spend a lot of money on paper.*

124

Listening

5 Underline the words so that the sentences express your opinion.

1. If you want to feel more energetic, then you should sleep **more / less.**
2. If you want to be more effective in business, you should use technology **more / less**.
3. To be more successful at work, work **longer / shorter** hours.
4. Eat **more / less** if you want to be healthier.

6 *PAIRS.* Compare your answers.

7 🎧 **Listen to the radio interview with Laura Chang, author of the book *Less Is More*. What does she think about the statements in Exercise 5?**

8 🎧 *PAIRS.* Listen again and answer the questions.

1. Why does the author think that people should work shorter hours?
2. What does the author say will happen if a person gets too little sleep? too much sleep?
3. Why does the author say people ought to try taking afternoon naps?

Grammar focus

1 **Study the examples with *should*, *could*, and *ought to*.**

> **(+)** She's exhausted! She **should work** shorter hours.
> He's so unhealthy. He really **ought to eat** less.
> If they need to use less energy, they could use fluorescent bulbs, or they **could get** solar hot water panels.
>
> **(–)** We **shouldn't sleep** so much on the weekends.
> We never get anything done!
>
> **(?)** I can't finish all my work. What **should I do**?

2 **Look at the examples again. Complete the rules in the chart with *could*, *should (not)*, or *ought to*.**

Modals *could*, *should (not)*, *ought to* for advice and suggestions
Use _____ and *ought to* for advice.
Use _____ for questions.
Use only _____ in questions to ask for advice and suggestions.
Use only _____ in negative for advice.
NOTE: *Ought to* is never used in the negative form.

(**Grammar Reference page 149**

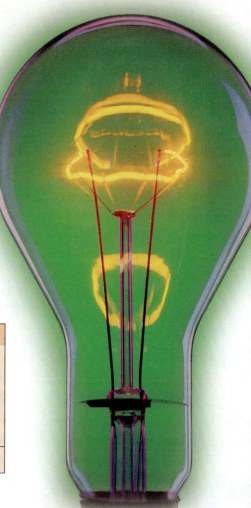

3 **Rewrite the sentences using the appropriate form of *should*, *could*, or *ought to*. More than one answer is possible in some cases.**

1. I want to have more energy. What is your advice?

   What should I do to have more energy?

2. One day the world will run out of oil, so it's important to invest in solar power now.

3. Don't use incandescent light bulbs. They waste a lot of resources.

4. To have more energy during the day, you have a couple of choices. Either sleep less at night, or take a nap in the afternoon.

5. If you want to save on your electric bill, here's my advice: use fluorescent bulbs as much as possible.

6. They need to get more done at work. What is your advice?

7. Don't leave the lights on if you're not in a room.

8. Here's a suggestion to do better at work: use less technology.

4 ***PAIRS.* Compare your answers.**

Pronunciation

5 🎧 **Listen. Notice the weak pronunciations of** *should* **and** *could* **and the linked pronunciation of** *ought to* **("oughta").**

What should I do?

You could take an afternoon nap.

You **ought to** relax more.

You should work shorter hours.

You could spend less time at the computer.

You **ought to** sleep less.

6 🎧 **Listen again and repeat.**

Speaking

7 *GROUPS OF 3.* **Describe a situation. Ask for and give advice. Student A, look at this page. Student B, look at page 137. Student C, look at page 140.**

Take turns sharing your problems and giving advice on what to do.

Student A

Problem #1
I can read and write English well, but when I try to have a conversation in English, I feel embarrassed. Do you have any suggestions?

Problem #4
It takes me too long to get to work and back home every day. I spend too much time commuting every day. Any ideas?

Problem #7
My colleagues at work always arrive late for meetings. I waste my time waiting for them. Help!

A: Maybe you should try . . .
B: Or, what about this? I think you should . . .

Writing

8 **Think of a problem that a friend or relative has. Write the person a short letter giving him or her advice on that problem. Use the modals** *should/shouldn't, could,* **and** *ought to* **for giving advice.**

CONVERSATION TO GO

A: What should I do?
B: You ought to relax more.

UNIT 28

Celebrate

Vocabulary Words related to parties
Grammar Present unreal conditional (*If* + simple past + *would* + verb)
Speaking Talking about imaginary situations

Lesson A

Getting started

1 Write the words and phrases from the box in the correct columns.

~~anniversary~~	barbecue	birthday	~~black tie~~
DJ	dinner	family reunion	graduation
live music	pianist	potluck dinner	wedding

Occasion	Type of party	Music
anniversary	black tie	

2 Complete the sentences with words from Exercise 1.

1. The company is having a _black tie_ party, so I guess I'll have to rent a tuxedo.

2. What are you taking to the _____ at Jack's house? I'm taking Thai chicken salad, my specialty!

3. _____ is always better than a DJ, don't you think?

4. I don't have _____ parties because I can't cook.

5. It's such a hot day. Let's have a _____ at the lake.

6. Jan's having a big _____ party in her backyard on Saturday. She's turning twenty-one on Friday.

7. My brother and I gave a party for my parents' twenty-fifth _____. All their friends and our family came.

3 *PAIRS.* Compare your answers.

128

Reading

4 A magazine is holding a competition. Read the advertisement and answer the questions.

1. Why is the magazine having a competition?
2. What do you have to do to enter?
3. What's the prize?

5 *PAIRS.* Match the sentences with the pictures below.

1. If we had a formal dinner with the family, my parents would love it. __B__

2. If it were possible, I would have fireworks. _____

3. I'd have a party on a yacht if money were not a problem. _____

4. If the children couldn't come, it wouldn't be a real family reunion. _____

5. If we had live music, people would have a great time. _____

6. I would not serve the food myself if I had the money to hire a waitress. _____

It's party time

Help us celebrate our

100th edition

Win the party of a lifetime for someone you love. We'll pay for everything.

All you have to do is tell us your party plans. If you had the chance to have the party of a lifetime, who would it be for, when would you have the party, and what would you celebrate?

If money were no problem,

- what type of party would it be?
- where would you have the party?
- what food and drink would you choose?
- how many people would you invite?

To enter the competition you must be 18 or over. The competition closes on December 31.

Ⓐ

Ⓑ

Grammar focus

1 **Study the examples of the present unreal conditional.**

> **(+) If** I **were** a millionaire, I**'d have** a party on a yacht.
> **(–)** It **wouldn't be** a family reunion **if** the children **couldn't come**.
> **(?) If** you **invited** all your friends to a party, where **would** it **be**?

2 **Look at the examples again. Underline the correct information to complete the rules in the chart.**

Present unreal conditional
Use the present unreal conditional to talk about **real / imaginary** situations.
The verb in the *if* clause is in the **base form / past tense**.
Use **would / should** in the result clause.
Use a comma when the *if* clause comes **first / last**.
NOTE: Use *were* for all forms of *be*.

> **Grammar Reference page 149**

3 **Rewrite the sentences using the present unreal conditional.**

1. I live in a small apartment, so I don't have large parties.
   If I didn't have a small apartment, I'd have large parties.
2. I don't have enough money, so I can't take a long vacation.
3. Etsu doesn't like to cook. She doesn't invite us to her house for dinner.
4. I don't have a barbecue every weekend only because I don't have a backyard.
5. Imad never invites his friends to his house because he lives too far out of town.
6. Magali is not a good dancer. That's why she doesn't go to clubs with her friends.
7. My neighbors complain about the noise, so I can't have a lot of parties.
8. A beach party is a great way to celebrate a birthday, but mine is in the winter.

Pronunciation

4 🎧 **Listen. Notice the pronunciation of the weak and contracted forms of *would*.**

Where **would** it be?

I**'d** have the party at a restaurant.

We**'d** have live music.

We**'d** dance all night.

If you could have a party, where **would** it be?

I **wouldn't** cook.

They**'d** play salsa.

Everyone **would** have a great time.

5 🎧 **Listen again and repeat.**

Speaking

6 **BEFORE YOU SPEAK.** What is your idea of a perfect party? Enter the competition. Take notes.

100th Edition "Party of a Lifetime"
Official Competition Entry Form

Place _____

Time/Occasion _____

Type of party _____

Food and drink _____

Music _____

Number of people _____

(Other ideas) _____

_____

_____

7 **GROUPS OF 3.** Tell each other about your party and answer questions about it. Then vote for the winning entry.

My party would be a surprise party for my boyfriend. It would be . . .

8 Tell the class about your party.

Writing

9 Write an invitation to the party you have arranged. Be creative and include information about the points on the list.

- occasion (reason for the party)
- type of party
- when and where the party is
- how to get there
- dress code (casual, elegant, . . .)

CONVERSATION TO GO

A: What **would** you **do if** you **won** a competition?
B: **If I won** a lot of money, **I'd throw** myself a big going-away party at work!

Unit 25 Arranged marriages

1 🎧 Listen to the model conversation.

2 *PAIRS.* What do you think makes a successful marriage? Use the phrases in the chart and your own ideas to make five statements expressing your opinion.

I think it's . . .	a good idea . . .	(for . . .) to . . .
	a bad idea . . .	get married
	crazy / absurd / wonderful . . .	get to know each other
	very / somewhat / not very important . . .	get engaged
		get upset
		get along
		get over something

Unit 26 Money matters

3 🎧 Listen to the model conversation.

4 *GROUPS OF 4.* Student A, you have just won a million dollars and you're trying to keep it a secret. Students B, C, and D, you've heard about Student A's winnings and are visiting him or her. Read your situation and then have a conversation. Keep talking until you reach an agreement.

Student A's situation: You're planning to have a family someday. You need this money to provide you and your family with financial security.

Student B's situation: You loaned Student A some money back in high school but he or she never paid you back. Now you want him or her to pay back what he or she owes—with interest!

Student C's situation: You have a great idea for a new business, but the bank won't give you a loan. You want Student A to invest some money in the business. He or she would be your partner.

Student D's situation: You were best friends with Student A when you were children. Now you are the president of a charity that helps feed hungry people all over the world. You want Student A to donate some of his or her money to this charity.

Unit 27 Less is more

5 🎧 Listen to the model conversation.

6 *PAIRS.* Role-play. You have one of the problems below. Use your imagination to add details. Take turns asking for and giving advice.

You . . .
    spend too much time working/sleeping/shopping . . .
    don't spend enough time with your family/at your work/with your friends . . .
    don't have enough space to work/exercise/cook . . .
    spend too much money on clothes/food/jewelry . . .
    waste too much time on the Internet/playing cards/watching TV . . .

Unit 28 Celebrate

7 🎧 Listen to the model conversation and look at the pictures.

8 *GROUPS OF 3.* Take turns asking and answering *what if* . . . questions about the situations below. Give reasons for your answers. Who has the most original idea?

- win a contest
- don't have to go to school or work every day
- don't need to worry about money
- can live anywhere in the world
- have all the free time you want
- have dinner with a famous person

World of Music 4

If I Could Turn Back Time
Cher

Vocabulary

1 **GROUPS OF 3.** **What do you think these sentences mean? Choose the best answer.**

1. I'd take back those words that hurt you.
   a. I'd return that book to the store if you don't like it.
   b. I wish I hadn't said those hurtful things to you.
   c. I wish I hadn't done those terrible things to you.
2. Pride's like a knife; it can cut deep inside.
   a. Sharp knives are dangerous.
   b. Pride is similar to a knife because they can both cut you.
   c. Pride is similar to a knife because they can both hurt people.
3. Words are like weapons; they wound sometimes.
   a. Words can hurt someone as badly as a weapon.
   b. People can injure others easily if they aren't careful.
   c. People need to be careful with weapons because they might wound someone.

Listening

2 🎧 **Listen to the song. Which word best describes the feelings of the speaker?**

a. regretful   b. worried   c. joyful

3 🎧 **Listen to the song and put each line of the chorus in order.**

4 **PAIRS.** **Compare your answers.**

Known for her outrageous costumes and wigs, Cher has faded from popularity many times over her long career but has always managed to emerge again into the limelight. "If I Could Turn Back Time" is one of Cher's many "comeback" songs.

Speaking

5 **GROUPS OF 3.** **Discuss the questions. Explain your opinions and ask and answer follow-up questions.**

1. What do you think the story behind this song might be?
2. What might have happened to make the singer feel the way she does?

If I Could Turn Back Time

If I could turn back time

If I could find a way

I'd take back those words that have hurt you and you'd stay

I don't know why I did the things I did

I don't know why I said the things I said

Pride's like a knife it can cut deep inside

Words are like weapons, they wound sometimes

I didn't really mean to hurt you

I didn't wanna see you go

I know I made you cry, but baby

CHORUS

back / time / if / could / turn / I _____

way / if / could / I / find / a _____

take / I'd / back / words / those / you / hurt / that _____

you'd / and / stay _____

I / the / reach / if / could/ stars _____

you / to / give / all / I'd / them _____

then you'd love me, love me,

used / do / to / you / like _____

I / time / back / if / could / turn _____

My world was shattered I was torn apart

Like someone took a knife and drove it

deep in my heart

You walked out that door I swore that I didn't care

but I lost everything darling then and there

Too strong to tell you I was sorry

CHORUS

Unit 1, Exercise 6
Student A

Student A, this is your situation. Complete each sentence with information that is true for you. Use your imagination and add at least two more details!

- You went to high school (secondary school) with Student B, but you haven't seen each other in a few years.
- You used to be an actor, but now you're working at _____.
- You're taking _____ classes.
- You're living in _____.
- _____
- _____
- Ask about Student B's job and what he or she is doing these days.
- End your conversation.

Unit 7, Exercise 4
Student B

Student B, your impressions of the restaurant include:

- atmosphere not formal enough—hard to have a conversation
- waiters couldn't answer questions, not knowledgeable enough about the menu items
- pizzas were too bland and fatty—not enough spices and too much cheese
- good salad, but dressing too sweet
- only offered soft drinks—no iced tea or hot beverages
- much too expensive

With your partner, decide if you would go back to that restaurant again.

A: I thought the salad was really fresh.
B: Yes, but I didn't like the dressing. I thought it was too sweet.
A: Really? I didn't think it was sweet enough. It seemed sour to me.

Unit 3, Exercise 4
Student B

Read the brochure. Then take turns asking and answering questions about the facilities and services at your partner's hotel. Both hotels cost $115 per night. Together, choose one of the hotels.

A: How many rooms does the Delta Hotel have?
B: It has 32 rooms. Does the Marina offer free airport transportation?

The Delta Hotel

A cozy, charming hotel located in the heart of downtown offering:

- free airport transportation
- 32 guest rooms, each decorated with antique furniture and paintings
- television and telephone in all rooms, with high-speed Internet access
- exercise room and sauna
- 24-hour coffee shop and café

Our concierge will be happy to assist you with theater or opera tickets and can recommend fine restaurants within walking distance of the hotel.

Review 6, Exercise 2
Student B

Role-play #1

Student A is your teacher. He or she is explaining a math problem, but you don't understand. Ask the teacher to explain it again.

Role-play #2

You get on a bus with your elderly grandmother. Student A is sitting in the seat near the door. You ask him or her to let your grandmother sit there.

Role-play #3

You are having a party with some friends. Student A is your neighbor. He or she comes to your door to ask you something.

Unit 4, Exercise 7
Student A

You're a patient. Don't give the doctor your information all at once. Try to make the doctor ask you questions to find out what your problem might be. Choose one of the following situations:

- **Situation 1:** You have the following symptoms: red eyes, itchy throat, runny nose, headache. You arrive at the doctor's office very tired and depressed.

- **Situation 2:** You have the following symptoms: You have a very bad rash on your hands and face. It's red and itchy and painful. You have had it for almost a week. You never drink coffee or tea or milk. You only eat chocolate on special occasions. You don't have any pets, but you did go horseback riding last weekend. You went to the zoo two weeks ago.

- **Situation 3:** Your choice. You choose the symptoms.

Unit 27, Exercise 7
Student B

Take turns sharing your problems and giving advice on what to do.

A: Maybe you should try . . .
B: Or, what about this? I think you should . . .

Problem #2

I have a computer at home, but I can't use it much because every time I try to download something, it tells me it's out of memory. What can I do?

Problem #5

I have no problem learning new English words in class, but after a day or two, I always forget the new words or what they mean. What would you suggest?

Problem #8

I feel that I'm not saving enough money. I want to spend less and save more, but how?

Unit 9, Exercise 6
Student A

You and Student B are taking a weekend trip to Washington, D.C., together. Ask Student B questions and fill in the missing itinerary information about your trip. Remember to use the simple present to ask for information about schedules, timetables, and events. Answer Student B's questions.

A: What airline are we on?
B: We're on . . .

WorldView Travel

Here is your itinerary. Have a great trip!

FLIGHT INFORMATION

Airline: <u>Jet Airways</u>   Ticket/class: _____

to Washington, D.C.   **from Washington, D.C.**

Day/date: Friday, April 19   Day/date: Sunday, April 21
Time departs: _____   Time departs: _____
Time arrives: _____   Time arrives: _____

HOTEL INFORMATION

The Wellington Hotel
(Located 5 blocks from the White House)

Arrival date: Friday, April 19   Check-in time: 1:00 P.M.
Departure date: Sunday, April 21   Check-out time: 11:00 A.M.
Free airport transfers

Unit 17, Exercise 5

3–4 *a* answers: You have very little willpower and find it difficult to control your mind and body. Try harder!

3–4 *b* answers: It is easy for you to achieve things by controlling your mind and body. You have a lot of willpower. Congratulations!

3–4 *c* answers: You are like most people . . . you have some willpower, but not enough. Don't give up!

Unit 1, Exercise 6
Student B

Student B, this is your situation. Complete each sentence with information that is true for you. Use your imagination and add at least two more details!

• You went to high school (secondary school) with Student A, but you haven't seen each other in a few years.
• You're a/an (your occupation). You're working at
  _____ .
• You're also taking _____ classes.
• _____
• _____
• Ask Student A where he or she is living now.
• Ask Student A if he or she is still acting.
• End your conversation.

Review 1, Exercise 8
Student B

Student B, use this information to answer Student A's questions.

Super Seven Hotel

• a budget motel with all the comforts of home
• just minutes from the airport
• 78 rooms ($59/night), all with television and telephone
• 24-hour coffee shop and café
• exercise room and sauna
• a conference room
• computer hookups and fax service available
• free baby-sitting service 24 hours a day

Unit 24, Exercise 4
Student A

Look at the cues and follow the model to make unfinished sentences using *who, that/which,* and *where.* Do not say the answer (in parentheses). Take turns saying your unfinished sentences to your group. The person who finishes it first with the correct answer gets 1 point.

A: *A person who flies planes is . . .*
B: *A pilot.*
A: *Correct. You get a point.*

1. person / flies planes
   (a pilot)
   A person who flies planes is . . .
2. machine / cooks food very fast
   (a microwave oven)
3. place / people store their books
   (a bookshelf)
4. movie / very scary
   (a horror movie)
5. man / getting married
   (a groom)
6. place / you can rent a room for a night
   (a hotel)

Unit 13, Exercise 8
Students A and B

You are a married couple in the U.S. Student A is from the U.S. Student B is from another country. Immigration officers are going to interview you both, but separately. You have five minutes to prepare for the interview. Work together to make sure you give the same information about:

• how long Student B has been in the U.S.
• how long you have known each other/been married
• where you met
• what your favorite thing about the other person is
• your wedding
• your jobs
• what you do in your free time

When the teacher calls "Time," go to page 63, Exercise 9.

Unit 8, Exercise 6
Student A

You are a very neat and responsible person. You enjoy cooking, you study a lot, and you always get to bed before 10:00 P.M. You wake up at 6:00 A.M. You love classical music.

These are some of the things you want your roommate to agree to. He or she has to:
• keep the house neat and clean
• take out the trash every day
• do his or her own laundry at least once a week
• take turns doing the housework
• pay 50% of all the bills

He or she can't:
• play loud music after 10:00 P.M.
• be late in paying the bills

Work out an agreement with your partner. Take notes on page 37.

You don't have to go to bed early, but you have to be quiet if you're up after ten, so you can't play loud music then.

Review 4, Exercise 2
Students A and B

1. **Students A and B, you are roommates. Prepare for a meeting with your new landlord.**

   Decide how long you've:
   lived in the U.S. _____
   known each other _____
   shared an apartment _____
   taken English classes together _____

2. **Ask these questions to find out whether or not Students C and D are really roommates.**

   How long have you:
   lived in the U.S.? _____
   known each other? _____
   shared an apartment? _____
   taken English classes together? _____
   had your dog? _____

Unit 9, Exercise 6
Student B

You and Student A are taking a weekend trip to Washington, D.C., together. Ask Student A questions and fill in the missing itinerary information about your trip. Remember to use the simple present to ask for information about schedules, timetables, and events. Answer Student A's questions.

A: What airline are we on?
B: We're on . . .

WorldView Travel

Here is your itinerary. Have a great trip!

FLIGHT INFORMATION

Airline: Jet Airways

to Washington, D.C.

Ticket/class: business class

from Washington, D.C.

Day/date: _____
Time departs: 7:00 A.M.
Time arrives: 12:00 noon

Day/date: _____
Time departs: 4:00 P.M.
Time arrives: 9:00 P.M.

HOTEL INFORMATION

The Wellington Hotel
(Located _____)
Arrival date: _____   Check-in time: _____
Departure date: _____   Check-out time: _____
Free airport transfers

Unit 13, Exercise 8
Students C and D

You are immigration officers in the U.S. Students A and B are married. Student A is from the U.S. Student B is from another country. You think they may not have a real marriage. You have five minutes to work together to prepare questions to ask the couple. You will ask Students A and B the same questions separately and then compare their answers. Write your questions on a piece of paper. Ask questions about:

- how long Student B has been in the country
- how long they have known each other/been married
- where they met
- what their favorite thing about the other person is
- their wedding (When? Where? How many people attended? How long it lasted?)
- their jobs
- what they do in their free time

When the Teacher calls "Time," go to page 63, Exercise 9.

Review 4, Exercise 2
Students C and D

1. Ask these questions to find out whether or not Students A and B are really roommates.

   How long have you:
   lived in the U.S.? _____
   known each other? _____
   shared an apartment? _____
   taken English classes together? _____
   worked at the same place? _____

2. Students C and D, you are roommates. Prepare for a meeting with your new landlord.

   Decide how long you've:
   lived in the U.S. _____
   known each other _____
   shared an apartment _____
   taken English classes together _____

Unit 22, Exercise 8
Student A

1. Read the text and ask Student B questions to find out the missing information.

A: What was stolen from a train?

In England in 1963, **(1)** _____ was stolen from a train. The crime was called **(2)** _____. The train was stopped near **(3)** _____. The driver was attacked, and the train was then driven one kilometer down the track. One hundred and twenty bags of bills were stolen. The money was taken **(4)** _____, where the robbers even used some of it to play Monopoly. But very soon, the thirteen main thieves were arrested, and most of the money was recovered.

2. Now answer Student B's questions.

Unit 27, Exercise 7
Student C

Take turns sharing your problems and giving advice on what to do.

A: Maybe you should try . . .
B: Or, what about this? I think you should . . .

Problem #3

I'm out of shape and need to do more exercise. But running seems a waste of energy. Any ideas?

Problem #6

I never remember my friends' birthdays. OK, it saves money on cards and presents. But what's the answer?

Problem #9

I like everyone in class, but I feel more comfortable working alone than with others. Do you have any suggestions?

Unit 24, Exercise 4
Student B

Look at the cues and follow the model to make unfinished sentences using *who*, *that*/*which*, and *where*. Do not say the answer (in parentheses). Take turns saying your unfinished sentences to your group. The person who finishes it first with the correct answer gets 1 point.

B: A person who writes with his or her left hand is . . .
C: A lefty.
B: Correct.

1. person / writes with his or her left hand
   (a lefty)
2. plastic thing / you use instead of money
   (a credit card)
3. place / you can see famous paintings
   (a museum)
4. movie / makes you laugh
   (a comedy)
5. place in a hotel / you check in
   (a lobby)
6. woman / getting married
   (a bride)

Review 1, Exercise 8
Student A

Student A, use this information to answer Student B's questions.

The Drake Hotel
• a classic hotel in the heart of the city
• 5 minutes from fabulous stores, restaurants, and museums
• free transportation to and from the airport
• 153 modern rooms ($219/night) and 25 guest suites ($359/night)
• satellite TV, computer and fax hook-ups in all rooms
• a large ballroom
• 2 conference rooms
• 24-hour business service and translation service
• a fitness center
• an award-winning restaurant and café

Unit 8, Exercise 6
Student B

You are not a very neat person. You have no idea how to cook. You always go out to restaurants, and you like to have fun. Often you don't come home until after midnight. You love rock and roll music and like to play it loud on your stereo.

These are some of the things you want your roommate to agree to. He or she has to:
• do the housework
• not make a fuss if your room is messy
• let you invite friends over for parties
• keep his or her CDs and tapes separate from yours
• let you play rock and roll anytime
• not worry if the bills don't get paid on time

He or she can't:
• make noise before noon
• expect you to be home for dinner

Work out an agreement with your partner. Take notes on page 37.

I'm usually out late, so you can't make noise before noon. You don't have to leave the house, you just have to be quiet.

Unit 22, Exercise 8
Student B

1. Read the text and answer Student A's questions.

In England, in 1963, almost four million dollars was stolen from a train. The crime was called the Great Train Robbery. The train was stopped near London. **(1)** _____ was attacked, and the train was then driven one kilometer down the track. **(2)** _____ bags of bills were stolen. The money was taken to a farm, where the robbers even used some of it to play Monopoly. But very soon, **(3)** _____ were arrested, and **(4)** _____ was recovered.

2. Now ask Student A questions to find out the missing information in your text.

Unit 24, Exercise 4
Student C

Look at the cues and follow the model to make unfinished sentences using *who*, *that/which*, and *where*. Do not say the answer (in parentheses). Take turns saying your unfinished sentence to your group. The person who finishes it first with the correct answer gets 1 point.

C: A movie that has lots of fights and explosions is . . .
B: A thriller.
C: No.
A: An action movie.
C: Correct. You get a point.

1. movie / has lots of fights and explosions
   (an action movie)
2. person / decorate homes or offices
   (an interior designer)
3. place / you go to work out
   (a fitness center)
4. person / tricks people into giving him or her money
   (a con artist)

5. TV program / usually involves love
   (a soap opera)
6. place / doctors and nurses work
   (a hospital)

Unit 21, Exercise 7
Student B

Role-play #1

Student A is your close friend. Listen and reply.

Role-play #2

You're in a new office and don't know where the light switches are. Ask a co-worker, Student A, to turn on the lights.

Role-play #3

Student A is your employee. Listen and reply.

Role-play #4

Your friends are visiting and want to listen to music. Ask your neighbor, Student A, if you can turn the volume up.

Grammar reference

Unit 1

Present continuous for the extended present

- Use the present continuous to talk about temporary events that are happening at this moment but that will be completed at some future time.
  *Halley's **taking** courses at the local college.*
  *She **isn't dating** anyone right now.*
  ***Are** you **walking** to the deli?*

Unit 2

Comparative adjectives, *as . . . as*

- Use the comparative form of adjectives with **than** to compare two things or people.

Adjective	Comparative form
one syllable	add *–er*
two syllable, ends with *–y*	change *y* to *i* and add *–er*
two syllables or more	use ***more*** + adjective
irregular (**good, bad**)	***better*** than, ***worse*** than

*Boys are **louder than** girls.*
*Boys are **messier than** girls.*
*Girls are **more talkative** than boys.*
*Girls are **better than** boys at school.*

- Use *as* + adjective + *as* to say there is no difference between two people or things.
  *Boys are **as smart as** girls.* (They have the same intelligence.)
  *Girls are **as polite as** boys.* (They have the same manners.)

- Use ***not as*** + adjective + ***as*** to say there is a difference between two people or things.
  *Masako is **not as fast as** Robert.* (Robert is faster.)
  *Elysse is not **as hardworking as** her brother.* (Her brother is more hardworking.)

Unit 3

Review: Simple present statements and questions

Affirmative		
I/You/We/They	like	to order room service.
He/She	like**s**	
Negative		
I/You/We/They	**don't**	have a room with an ocean view.
He/She/It	**doesn't**	
***Yes/No* question**		
Do	I/you/we/they	prefer a room with a balcony?
Does	he/she/it	
Short answer		
Yes,	I/you/we/they	**do**.
	he/she/it	**does**.
No,	I/you/we/they	**don't**.
	he/she/it	**doesn't**.

Wh– question				
What	**do**	I/you	base form of the verb	?
When				
Where	**does**	he/she/it		
Why				
How	**do**	we/they		

*Where **do** I **get** towels for the pool?*
*When **does** the restaurant **serve** breakfast?*
*Why **do** the premier suites **cost** more than the double deluxe rooms?*

Unit 4

Adjectives ending in *–ed* and *–ing*

- Use adjectives ending in *–ed* to describe the way a person feels.
  *Marissa is **annoyed**.* (She looks angry or upset.)
  *Luke was **shocked**.* (He looked very surprised.)
  *Jalil felt **embarrassed**.* (His face turned red.)

- Use adjectives ending in *–ing* to explain what or who makes a person feel a certain way.
  *Her allergies are **annoying**.* (They bother her.)
  *The news was **shocking** to Luke.* (He didn't expect it.)
  *The situation was **embarrassing**.* (Everyone stared at Jalil.)

Grammar reference

Unit 5

Subject and object questions

- The subject of a sentence does the action. The object of a sentence receives the action.

- When **who** is the subject of the question, put it before the verb. Don't use *do/does*.
  Who helps Ron? Mary does.
  Who sings the singing telegrams? Ron does.
  Who pays the agency? People who order telegrams do.
  (*Who* is the subject of these questions.)

- When **who** is the object of a question, use normal question word order and *do/does*.
  Who does Mary help? Mary helps Ron.
  Who does Ron sing to? He sings to people at parties.
  Who do people pay? They pay the agency.
  (*Who* is the object of these questions.)

Unit 6

Review: simple past vs. past continuous

- Use the simple past to talk about completed actions in the past, often with a time reference (*yesterday, last week, in 1999,* etc.).
  We **went** to Ireland on vacation **in 2003**.
  I **didn't go** on vacation **last year**.
  Did you **go** to the beach **in July**?

- Use the past continuous to talk about actions that continued for a period of time in the past.
  It **was raining** almost the whole time.
  People **weren't doing** much outside.
  Were you **considering** leaving early?

- Use the past continuous to set the scene in a story.
  The rain **was falling** and the wind **was blowing** through the trees in the dark forest . . .

- Use the simple past and past continuous together in one sentence if the first action was still going on when the second action happened.
  It **was raining** when suddenly the sun **came** through the clouds.
  We **weren't paying** attention when we **passed** the restaurant.
  What **were** you **doing** when you **heard** the news?

Unit 7

Too, enough

- Use **too** followed by an adjective to say "more than is needed or wanted."
  The restaurant was **too** noisy. (We couldn't hear because of the noise.)
  Is it **too** cold in here? (Is the temperature lower than you want?)

- Use an adjective followed by **enough** to say "as much as necessary or wanted."
  The desserts are sweet **enough**. (They don't need to be sweeter.)
  The food wasn't spicy **enough**. (It needed more spices.)
  Is the tea hot **enough**? (Does it need to be hotter?)

Notes:
- Do not put the adjective after **enough**.
  X *The water is enough cold.*
- Use **too** and **enough** with adverbs.
  *He cooks **too plainly** for my taste.*
  *We didn't follow the recipe **carefully enough**.*

Use **enough** followed by a noun to say "as much as necessary or wanted."
There is **enough** sauce on the pasta. (I don't want more.)
My coffee doesn't have **enough** sugar. (It needs more.)
Did you get **enough** salad? (Did you get all the salad that you wanted?)

Unit 8

Modals: *have to/don't have to, must, can't* for obligation and prohibition

- Use **must** to say that something is necessary.
  She **must** sign a prenuptial agreement before they get married. (He won't marry her if she doesn't.)
  He **must** give her $2,000 per month. (It's in the prenuptial agreement.)

- Also use **have / has to** to say that something is necessary.
  John **has to** pay $10,000. (That's what the contract says.)
  Do I **have to** wait for you? (Is it necessary to wait?)

- Use **don't have to** to say that something isn't necessary.
  *They **don't have to** wash the dishes by hand.* (They have a dishwasher.)
  *He **doesn't have to** pay the bills.* (His wife pays them.)

- Use **can't** to say that something is prohibited.
  *He **can't** ask her for any money.* (He's not allowed to ask for money.)
  *You **can't** get married in any state if you are under 16 years old.* (It is illegal.)

Unit 9

Simple present and present continuous for future

- Use the simple present to talk about schedules, timetables, and events in the future.
  *The tour **starts** at 7:30 tomorrow.*
  *The movie **isn't** over until 8:00.*
  ***Does** the boat **leave** at 6:00?*

- Use the present continuous to talk about personal plans in the future.
  *I**'m seeing** the doctor at 4:00.*
  *We**'re not going** to the movies tonight, but we**'re going** tomorrow.*
  ***Are** you **leaving** in the morning or the afternoon?*

Unit 10

Modal verbs for ability

- Use **can/can't** to talk about ability in the present.
  *I **can** write with both hands.*
  *You **can't** draw with your left hand.*
  ***Can** Jane cut with her right hand?*

- Use **could/couldn't** or **be able to** to talk about abilities that began at a specific moment or lasted for a period of time in the past.
  *I **could** read when I was four.*
  *Sam **couldn't** write very well.*
  ***Could** you run fast when you were a child?*
  *She **was able to** write her name before going to school.*
  *Franklin **wasn't able to** ride a bike until he was ten.*
  *When **were** your children **able to** walk?*

- Use **be able to** or **managed to** to talk about ability on a specific occasion in the past.
  *It was difficult, but we **were able to** fix the car.*
  *I **managed to** escape out the window.*
  ***Were** they **able to** find the exit.*
  ***Did** they **manage to** find the exit?*

- Use **not be able to**, **didn't manage to**, or **couldn't** to talk something that wasn't possible on a specific occasion in the past.
  *We tried, but we **weren't able to** fix the car.*
  *I **didn't manage to** escape. I had to be rescued.*
  *They **couldn't find** the exit. They had to ask someone where it was.*

Unit 11

Present perfect for indefinite past

- Use the present perfect to talk about actions that happened in the past when knowing the time of the action is not important.

Affirmative	subject + **have/has** + past participle *We've polished the floorboards.*
Negative	subject + **haven't/hasn't** + past participle *He hasn't removed the fireplace.*
Question	**have/has** + subject + past participle **Have** they **changed** the sofa covers?
Short answers	**Yes** + subject + **have/has** *Yes, they **have**.*
	No + subject + **haven't/hasn't** *No, they **haven't**.*

Note: Add **–ed** to regular verbs to form the past participle. See page 150 for a list of irregular verbs.

Grammar reference

Unit 12

Modals: *may, might, could* for possibility

- Use *may*, *might*, or *could* to talk about something that is possible in the future.
  *The group **may** stay in two different hotels.* (It's possible that they won't all stay in the same hotel.)
  *The guide **might** change the time of the tour.* (It's possible that she'll change the time.)
  *We **could** take a bus at 4:30, or we **could** wait until 6:00.* (Two options are both possible: the 4:30 bus and the 6:00 bus.)

- Use *may not* and *might not* to talk about something that probably won't happen in the future.
  *We **may not** have time to eat before we leave.* (There is a possibility that we won't have time to eat.)
  *The weather is going to be cloudy, but it **might not** rain.* (There is a possibility that it won't rain.)

- Use *couldn't* to talk about something that is not possible in the future.
  *I **couldn't** spend that much money on a trip.* (I wouldn't have any money left.)
  *She **couldn't** go on that trip.* (They are going to fly, and she hates airplanes.)

Unit 13

Review: present perfect with *for* and *since*

- Use the present perfect with *for* or *since* to talk about actions that started in the past and continue into the present.
  *I've **lived** in the United States **for** eight months.* (I moved here eight months ago. I still live here now.)
  *Peter **hasn't had** a pet **since** his dog died.* (After his dog died, he didn't have a pet. He still doesn't have a pet now.)
  ***Has** Sam **known** Claire **since** he was twenty?* (Did he meet her when he was twenty? Does he still know her?)

- Use the present perfect with *for* to talk about a length of time.
  *She's **dated** him **for** two weeks.*
  *He **hasn't lived** in New York **for** a long time.*
  ***Have** they **worked** together **for** ten years?*

- Use the present perfect with *since* to talk about a specific time that a continuing action started.
  *They've **been** in there **since** 2:00.*
  *He **hasn't talked** to us **since** Tuesday.*
  ***Have** you **been** married **since** 2002?*

Unit 14

Modals: *must, might, can't* for deduction

- Use *must* if you're very sure that something is true.
  *You've traveled all night. You **must** be tired!*
  *He's eating two sandwiches. He **must** be hungry.*

- Use *might* if you are not sure if something is true.
  *Your car keys **might** be on the kitchen table.* (Sometimes you put them there.)
  *They **might** be listening to music.* (They are wearing headphones.)

- Use *can't* if you are very sure that something isn't true.
  *That woman looks like Carly, but it **can't** be her.* (Carly is in Japan right now.)
  *Edena **can't** be happy.* (She just received bad news).

Unit 15

Will/won't for future and predictions

- Use *will* and *won't* to talk about the future.
  *Sanjay and Nina **will** get married.*
  *Nina's parents **won't** be happy.*

- Use *think* and *don't think* followed by a subject + *will* to make predictions.
  *I **think** Nina **will** convince her parents.*
  *I **don't think** they **will** cause any problems.*
  *Nina **thinks** they will have children someday.*
  *She **doesn't think** they'll live in London forever.*

Unit 16

Future real conditional (*If* + simple present + *will*)

- Use two clauses to make future real conditional statements.

If clause	Result clause
if + simple present	*will/won't* + base form of the verb

- Use the future real conditional to talk about things that may happen in the future and their results.
  *If you **eat** this cereal, you'**ll** be strong and healthy.*
  *If you **don't hurry**, we'**ll** be late.*
  *If I **call** you tonight, **will you** be home?*

- The *if* clause is often in the first position in a sentence, but it can also go second.
  *He'**ll** fix the washing machine **if** it **breaks**.*

Unit 17

Verbs + gerund and verbs + infinitive

- Use an infinitive after these verbs: **decide, learn, need, promise, want**.
  *I **want to go** out tonight.*
  *José doesn't **need to buy** any new clothes.*
  *Have you **decided to start** a diet?*

- Use a gerund after these verbs: **cut down on, dislike, enjoy, get out of, give up, keep on, practice, quit, stop, take up**.
  *We **gave up eating** meat.*
  *I **don't enjoy cooking**.*
  *Is Karen **taking up swimming**?*

Notes:
- Gerund = base form of the verb + **–ing**
- Infinitive = **to** + base form of the verb

Unit 18

Used to and would

- Use **used to/would** + base form of the verb to talk about repeated actions in the past that don't happen now.
  *A lot of people **used to waste** energy (but now they don't).*
  *They **didn't use to recycle** most materials.*
  ***Did** you **use to buy** cars that used a lot of gas?*
  *I'**d use** things once and throw them away.*
  *We **wouldn't turn** down the heat at night.*

- Use **used to** + base form of the verb to talk about states in the past that aren't that way now.
  *Energy sources **used to seem** endless.*
  *People **didn't use to know** that they were hurting the environment.*
  ***Did** she **use to think** that recycling was important?*

Unit 19

Passive (simple present)

- Use the passive when:
  - you're not interested in who or what does the action.
  - it's not important who or what does the action.
  - you don't know who or what does the action.

- The object of an active sentence becomes the subject of a passive sentence.
  *People make **the boxes**.*   (active)
  ***The boxes** are made.*   (passive)

Simple present passive
subject + **am/is/are** + past participle
The boxes **are made** in Morocco.
They **are sold** for $75.
The wood **is cut** by hand.
How **are** the boxes **made**? They **are made** by hand.

Unit 20

So, too, either, neither

- Use **so** and **too** to make additions to affirmative statements.
  *He was surprised by the ending, and I was, **too**.*
  *He was surprised by the ending, and **so was** I.*

- Use **not** + **either** and **neither** to make additions to negative statements.
  *The acting wasn't great, and the story wasn't **either**.*
  *The acting wasn't great, and **neither** was the story.*

- Place the auxiliary, modal, or form of **be** or **do** before the subject in an addition with **so** or **neither**.

- Always use an auxiliary, a modal, or a form of **be** or **do** to make an addition. In the addition, use the appropriate form of the same auxiliary, modal, **be**, or **do** that appears in the statement.
  *Renée Zellweger starred in the movie Chicago, and **so did** Catherine Zeta-Jones.*
  *She **is** a big fan of Keanu Reeves, and I **am, too**.*
  *Star Wars **didn't** make as much money as Titanic, and E.T. **didn't either**.*
  *Ben Affleck wasn't in The Lord of the Rings, and **neither was** Leonardo DiCaprio.*

Grammar reference

Unit 21

Modals: *could you, would you, would you mind . . . ?* for polite requests

- Use ***could you*** and ***would you*** followed by the base form of the verb to make polite requests.

Could you	open the window?	Of course.
	please turn off the lights?	
	make less noise?	
Would you	turn up the volume?	Sure.
	stop doing that, please?	

- You can also use ***would you mind*** followed by a gerund to make polite requests.

Would you mind	closing the door?	No, of course not.
	please turn on the lights?	
	speaking louder?	
	turning down the volume?	
	continuing that, please?	Not at all.

Unit 22

Passive (simple past)

- Use the simple past passive when the action is more important than the person or thing that did the action.

Simple past passive
Subject + ***was/were*** + past participle
The cars ***were stolen*** on Tuesday.
A window ***was broken.***

- The object of an active sentence becomes the subject of the passive sentence.
  *Someone found **my wallet**.*
  My wallet *was found.*

- Use ***by*** + the person or thing to say who or what did the action.
  *The manager **was hurt by** the robber.*
  *The building **wasn't hit by** lightning.*
  *What **was** the car **hit by**?*

Unit 23

Review: verbs for likes/dislikes followed by gerunds and/or infinitives

- Use a gerund or an infinitive after these verbs: ***like***, ***hate***, ***love***, and ***can('t) stand***.
  *I **like to go** to the gym, but I **hate to lift** weights.*
  *She **likes doing** aerobics, but she **hates running**.*
  *We **love to eat** fatty foods, but we **can't stand to gain weight**!*
  *They **love exercising** outside, but they **hate getting** a sunburn.*

- Use only a gerund after these verbs and phrasal verbs: ***mind***, ***enjoy***, ***be sick of***, and ***be into***.
  *I don't **mind walking**; it's good exercise!*
  *Do you **enjoy working** out?*
  *He was **sick of taking** the same kinds of classes at the gym, and now he**'s into doing** Pilates.*

Unit 24

Relative clauses with *that, which, who,* and *where*

- Use relative clauses with ***that***, ***which***, ***who***, and ***where*** to define people, places, and things.
  *A producer is someone **who** makes TV programs.*
  *This is the computer **which** we saw at the first store.*
  *A cell phone is something **that** makes communication convenient.*
  *A garage is a place **where** you can park a car.*

- Use ***who*** or ***that*** for people, ***which*** or ***that*** for things, and ***where*** for places.

Unit 25

It's **+ adjective/noun + infinitive to express opinion**

- Use ***It's*** followed by an adjective or a noun phrase and an infinitive to express an opinion. You can add ***for*** + an object after the adjective or noun phrase, but it's not necessary.

It's	absurd	(***for*** + people) to get married.
	crazy	
	important	
	wonderful	
	a good idea	
	a bad idea	

It's a good idea **to discuss** issues before marriage.
It's a good idea **for couples to discuss** issues before marriage.
It's important **to compromise** in a marriage.
It's important **for people to compromise** in a marriage.

Unit 26

Verbs with two objects

• Some verbs can have a direct object. A direct object receives the action of the verb. A direct object answers the question **what** or **who**.
*I received **my bank statement**.* (What did I receive? My bank statement.)
*The accountant didn't return **her call**.* (What didn't he return? The call.)
*When did you see **her**?* (Who did you see? Her.)

• Some verbs can also have an indirect object. An indirect object can come before the direct object. It answers the question *to whom* or *for whom*. The indirect object is usually a person.
*We offer **customers** first-class service.* (Who do we offer service to? Customers.)
*He doesn't owe **the accountant** money.* (Who doesn't he owe the money to? The accountant.)
*Did the bank send **you** a letter?* (Who was the letter for? You.)

• Use **to** or **for** + the indirect object when it follows the direct object.
*We offer first-class service **to customers**.*
*He doesn't owe money **to the accountant**.*
*Did the bank send a letter **to you**?*

Note: You can never have an indirect object without a direct object.
X I gave my accountant.

Unit 27

Review: Modals: *should/shouldn't, could, ought to* for advice

• Use **should, could,** or **ought to** tell someone you think something is a good idea.
*You **should** get more sleep.*
*We **could** try going to bed earlier.*
*They **ought to** do more exercise during the day.*

• Use **should** to ask for advice.
*What **should** I do?*
*What time **should** we leave?*

• Use **shouldn't** to tell someone you think something is a bad idea.
*You **shouldn't** work so hard.*
*We **shouldn't** wait too long.*

Unit 28

Present unreal conditional (*If* + simple past + *would* + verb)

• Use two clauses to make present unreal conditional statements.

If clause	Result clause
if + simple past	*would/wouldn't* + base form of the verb

• Use the present unreal conditional to talk about unreal events or conditions in the present and their results.
*If I **had** a million dollars, I'**d** throw a huge party.*
*If her hip **didn't hurt**, Grandma **would** dance.*
*If it **weren't** so far away, we'**d** all go to your house.*
***Would** you come to the party **if** you **had** time?*

• The **if** clause is often in the first position in a sentence, but it can also go second.
*It **wouldn't** be difficult **if** everyone **helped** out.*

Note: Always use the **were** form of the verb **be** in the **if** clause with the present unreal conditional.
*If I **were** you . . .*
*If she **were** nicer . . .*
*If they **weren't** so tired . . .*

Grammar reference

Irregular Verbs

Simple present	Simple past	Past Participle
be	was/were	been
become	became	become
begin	began	begun
break	broke	broken
build	built	built
buy	bought	bought
catch	caught	caught
choose	chose	chosen
come	came	come
cost	cost	cost
do	did	done
draw	drew	drawn
drink	drank	drunk
drive	drove	driven
eat	ate	eaten
fall	fell	fallen
feel	felt	felt
fight	fought	fought
find	found	found
fly	flew	flown
forget	forgot	forgotten
get	got	gotten
give	gave	given
go	went	gone
grow	grew	grown
hang	hung	hung
have	had	had
hear	heard	heard
hurt	hurt	hurt
keep	kept	kept
know	knew	known
leave	left	left
lend	lent	lent

Simple present	Simple past	Past Participle
lose	lost	lost
make	made	made
mean	meant	meant
meet	met	met
pay	paid	paid
put	put	put
quit	quit	quit
read	read	read
ride	rode	ridden
run	ran	run
say	said	said
see	saw	seen
sell	sold	sold
send	sent	sent
shake	shook	shaken
show	showed	shown
sing	sang	sung
sit	sat	sat
sleep	slept	slept
speak	spoke	spoken
spend	spent	spent
stand	stood	stood
swim	swam	swum
take	took	taken
teach	taught	taught
tell	told	told
think	thought	thought
throw	threw	thrown
understand	understood	understood
wear	wore	worn
win	won	won
write	wrote	written

Vocabulary

Unit 1
complimenting
ending a conversation
greeting
introducing
making conversation
small talk

Unit 2
aggressive
cooperative
competitive
emotional
hardworking
messy
noisy
talkative

Unit 3
thirteen/thirty
fourteen/forty
fifteen/fifty
sixteen/sixty
seventeen/seventy
eighteen/eighty
nineteen/ninety

baby-sitting service
business center
ballroom
café
casino
conference room
fitness center
guest room
limousine service
lobby
restaurant
sauna
swimming pool
tennis court
video arcade

Unit 4
backache
cold
earache
headache
rash

sore throat
stomachache

Unit 5
deliver   a telegram
hire   a person
make   breakfast
pay   bills
send   a greeting card
spend   time
take   pictures
take out   the trash

Unit 6
awful
bad
big
boiling
cold
crowded
enormous
exhausted
fantastic
fascinating
freezing
good
hot
interesting
packed
tired

absolutely
really
very

Unit 7
casual
courteous
elegant
formal
indifferent
polite
romantic
rude

bland
greasy
healthful
hot
low-fat

nutritious
salty
sour
spicy
sweet

Unit 8
lose their temper
do the housework
make prenuptial agreements
have some kind of insurance
take care of financial obligations
sign a contract
react to problems
exchange wedding rings

Unit 9
break down
get off
go on
head out
put someone up
show someone around
start off

Unit 10
a piece of cake
challenging
complicated
doable
hard
impossible
manageable
no trouble
simple
straightforward
tough

Unit 11
armchair
basket
bookcase
cabinet
carpet
drapes
fireplace
lamp
magazine rack
picture
plants

rug
sofa
stereo speakers
throw pillow
window

Unit 12

at + (a specific time)
at noon
in the evening
last night
last Sunday
next Sunday
on Sunday
on Sunday morning
this Sunday
yesterday afternoon

Unit 13

green card
ID (identification) card
immigration
nationalities
passport
permanent resident
tourist visa
work permit

Unit 14

cheer
clap
cry
laugh
scream
shout
whistle
yawn

Unit 15

crime
death
family life
greed
illness
marriage
misfortune
money
power
romance

Unit 16

clean
delicious
fast
fresh
healthy
reliable
safe
shiny
soft

Unit 17

cut back on
cut down on
get out of
give up
keep on
take up
throw away
turn down

Unit 18

alternative medicine
genetic engineering
hybrid cars
instant messaging
renewable resources
telecommuting
vegetarianism

Unit 19

cotton
glass
gold
leather
pewter
lycra
silver
wood

accessories
bathing suit
bicycling shorts
box
candlesticks
clothes/clothing
dress
earrings
gloves

jewelry
mirror
picture frame
ring
sandals
shirt
tray
vase
watch

Unit 20

action movie
animated film
comedy
drama
horror movie
martial arts film
musical
science fiction movie
thriller
western

Unit 21

go off
switch off
switch over to
turn down
turn off
turn on
turn up

Unit 22

robbery/robber/rob
burglary/burglar/burglarize
mugging/mugger/mug
scam/con artist/scam
shoplifting/shoplifter/shoplift
theft/thief/steal

get arrested
go to prison
pay a fine
do community service

Unit 23

take a break
take it easy
take off
take on
take part in
take up

Unit 24

cell phone
computer
digital camera
digital TV
DVD player
laptop
printer
scanner

Unit 25

best man
bride
bridesmaids
ceremony
groom
groomsmen
honeymoon
maid of honor
reception

get along
get back with
get divorced
get engaged
get married
get on each other's nerves
get over
get to know
get upset

Unit 26

bank account
bank statement
be in the black/red
borrow money
checking account
deposit money
invest money
lend money
pay interest
receive interest
save money
savings account
withdraw money

Unit 27

save energy
save money
save paper
save resources
save space
save time
spend money
spend time
use electricity
use money
use paper
use resources
use space
use time
waste electricity/energy
waste money
waste opportunities
waste paper
waste resources
waste space
waste time

Unit 28

anniversary
barbecue
birthday
black tie
DJ
dinner
family reunion
graduation
live music
pianist
potluck dinner
wedding

SINGLE PC LICENSE AGREEMENT AND LIMITED WARRANTY

How to Start the CD-ROM
This CD-ROM does not require an installation. The CD-ROM must be in the CD-ROM drive while using the program.

For Windows:
1. For optimal display, we recommend that your monitor be set with 800 x 600 resolution.
2. Insert the CD-ROM into the computer's CD-ROM drive.
3. The program should begin automatically.
4. If the program does not begin automatically, open "My Computer," and then double-click on the *WorldView* CD-ROM icon.

For Macintosh:
1. For optimal display, we recommend that your monitor be set with 800 x 600 resolution.
2. Insert the CD-ROM into the computer's CD-ROM drive.
3. Double-click on the CD-ROM icon on the computer's desktop.
4. Double-click on the WorldView file within the CD-ROM window.

System Requirements

For Windows 98
- Intel Pentium processor – min 300 MHz
- 64 MB RAM minimum
- CD-ROM drive
- Monitor resolution of 800 x 600 or higher
- Sound card, speakers, and microphone

For Windows XP, 2000
- Intel Pentium processor – min 400 MHz
- 128 MB RAM minimum
- CD-ROM drive
- Monitor resolution of 800 x 600 or higher
- Sound card, speakers, and microphone

For Macintosh
- PowerPC processor – minimum 300 MHz
- MacOS OSX
- 64 MB free RAM minimum
- CD-ROM drive
- Monitor resolution of 800 x 600 or higher
- Sound card, speakers, and microphone